reliable roses

reliable roses

Philip Harkness

Photography by Steve Wooster

Firefly Books

A FIREFLY BOOK

Published by Firefly Books Ltd. 2004
Copyright © 2004 Philip Harkness

All rights reserved. No part of this publication may be reproduced, stored in a retrieval system, or transmitted in any form or by any means, electronic, mechanical, photocopying, recording or otherwise, without the prior written permission of the Publisher.

First Printing

Publisher Cataloguing-in-Publication Data (U.S.)
(Library of Congress Standards)

Harkness,
Reliable roses : easy-to-grow roses that won't let you down / Harkness ; photography by Steve Wooster.
_1st ed.
[144] p. : col. photos. ; cm.
Includes index.
Summary: Garden guide to roses which covers selecting varieties, garden planning and designing, planting, growing cycles, pruning, maintenance, and growing zones. Includes rose directory identifying 75 different varieties.
ISBN 1-55297-893-1
1. Roses. 2. Rose culture. 3. Rose ----- Varieties. I. Wooster, Steve. II. Title.
635.9/ 3334 21 SB411.H325 2004

National Library of Canada Cataloguing in Publication

Harkness, Philip
Reliable roses : easy-to-grow roses that won't let you down / Philip Harkness; photography by Steve Wooster.
Includes index.
ISBN 1-55297-893-1 (bound).--ISBN 1-55297-892-3 (pbk.)
1. Roses. 2. Rose culture. I. Wooster, Steven II. Title.
SB411.H36 2004 635.9'33734
C2003-905310-5

Published in the United States in 2004 by
Firefly Books (U.S.) Inc.
P.O. Box 1338, Ellicott Station
Buffalo, New York 14205

Published in Canada in 2004 by
Firefly Books Ltd.
3680 Victoria Park Avenue
Toronto, Ontario, M2H 3K1

Color reproduction by Classic Scan, Singapore
Printed in China by Imago

Contents

Introduction

Roses are wonderful plants that nature has adorned with many beautiful features. In this book I aim to explore ways of enjoying roses and to investigate the best way of achieving good results without spending too much time in the garden. My approach is based on the fact that there are two important aspects to growing and enjoying roses.

Firstly, roses are planted in the garden for recreation, fun and pleasure. We should not be ashamed that our pursuit is hedonistic.

Secondly, to make our rose growing successful we should, wherever possible, try to work with nature and never against it.

In practical terms, this book is designed to make growing roses easier and more fun. The book will help you to use the strengths that nature provides to reduce problems in the cultivation of plants. It will not be a technical "tour de force" laden with history, science, genetics or botanical classification. There will not be in-depth discussion on the pathological makeup of the plant or the implications of applying chemicals. We are here for enjoyment at its most basic level, which we recognize as that which nature bestowed on the rose family and, with nature's help, we will enhance and tailor that beauty for our own gratification.

In this book there is a selection of varieties that you may wish to try in your garden. The selection of a good rose is subjective. If it provides the features that you deem to be important in a way that gives you pleasure, then it is a good rose for you, and that is all that is important. There are a mixture of types, some old and some new. Very few have no faults, but all have good qualities. I hope that this selection will introduce you to the vast variety of different shapes and forms available in the modern marketplace.

Our introduction to this adventure is to look at the diversity of the rose family. What nature began, man has improved, developing the rose's beautiful features further. Today we are able to enjoy the rose in myriad forms.

Left: The rose is extremely versatile and capable _ use it in mixed plantings in cottage gardens or formal settings.

Above: Make a feature by using climbing roses over a structure.

The rose family includes plants that grow happily as miniatures, never more than 12 to 15 in (30 to 38 cm) tall: neat compact plants, miniature in leaf, flower and form. At the other extreme there are rampant climbing and rambling roses. It is not unusual to find plants capable of extending to more than 30 ft (9 m). In between, there are roses that make perfect garden plants – something suitable for every garden and every taste.

With such an overwhelming choice of size, style and type it is hard to know where to start. There is a niche in every garden for the climbing and rambling roses. Watch them cover a fence, building or pergola. Enjoy the spectacular effect of a rose flowering high in a deciduous or evergreen tree. Equally, roses categorized as ground covers are easy to place in the garden, to prevent an influx of weeds, provide color and, most of all, be easy to maintain.

There are patio and border varieties. Growing taller than miniatures, but smaller than bush roses, they are always worth a try in tubs, planters and in borders.

Bush roses are subdivided into hybrid tea (large flowers), floribunda (cluster flowers) and grandiflora (taller, usually with clusters of flowers). All are great garden plants. They flower for a long time, repeat flowering throughout summer to early winter. As plants they can range from 3 ft (1 m) tall to at least 6 ft (1.8 m). There are only two important aspects to remember when buying; do I like them? And where will they go in my garden? Beyond that there is no logical reason to have a prejudice. If you answer the first question with a yes, then it is irrelevant whether it is classified as a hybrid tea or floribunda. It is only blinkered dogma that allows you to say, "Yes I like it," only to discover it is a floribunda and then say, "I don't like it, as I don't like floribundas." Have an open mind and do not let irrelevant classifications and labels cloud your judgment.

The final grouping of roses is shrub roses. This term covers all that is left. Many are modern varieties, others old and some ancient, the species that all modern roses have evolved from. As a generalization they will grow bigger and wider than bush roses, between 6 and 12 ft (1.8 and 3.7 m) tall by up to 8 ft (2.5 m) wide in some examples. Needless to say there are many varieties of shrub roses that are smaller than these dimensions – always check mature height information carefully before purchasing. The second generalization is that the older shrub roses will flower only once in summer, while most of the modern ones will repeat bloom.

These outlines, in the most basic form, only touch the surface of how the plant may grow. Within each range of roses there will be flowers of all different shapes and sizes. A rose can produce a flower with a minimum of five petals, known as a single flower; or 10 to 15 petals, a semi-double flower. At the other extreme there may be up to a hundred petals in one flower. To fall in with convention, but not to be very helpful, those with 20 petals upwards are referred to as double flowers, so one term covers a wide range of blooms. Flowers can range from less than 1 in (2.5 cm) across to more than 5 in (13 cm) across. There are so many permutations that there is always a rose somewhere to appeal to every individual.

But this is only touching on the look of the flower. There is the magic chemistry cannot copy: the range of satisfying rose perfumes. Our noses can have as much pleasure as our eyes. Perfumes range from light to heady, sweet to spicy; there may be hints of apple, honey or citronella to name a few.

As we get to know the rose, we will understand that it is a hardy and resilient garden plant. Roses withstand a vast range of ambient and climatic conditions. Some thrive in shady sites, others prefer sunlight; but all will enjoy positions with moderate or above average sunlight. Some roses are winter hardy to temperatures of 14°F (–10°C), others

Below: Roses can lengthen the flowering season of mixed plantings, and add glorious perfume.

Right: Some of the most beautiful of all climbing plants are roses.

will suffer. All withstand lower winter temperatures if they are protected from cold winds. In this book, zones are used to indicate hardiness, referring to regions in North America.

This book is written with the hope that it will encourage love and appreciation of the rose. It will act as a guide to help dispel myths, to understand intricacies but, most of all, to show how easy it is to grow and enjoy roses.

Easy Road to Perfect Roses

Nature's Elements

This chapter title is a misnomer. There are areas in which there are no shortcuts and the only way to achieve good results is by old-fashioned hard work. The trick is to assess the strengths that nature has provided and to utilize them.

The first requirement is to define our personal goals. We all want the best results possible but we must put the term "best results" into our personal context. For every gardener there is a different answer. Are you looking for perfection, with no damage from insects or disease? Do you tolerate some imperfections, not getting stressed out over an insect attack or low-level disease? Do you manage your garden in a wholly organic natural way, without artificial chemicals of any sort? Whatever is important to you, some of the ideas here will help you increase the pleasure your roses give to you.

In a garden the elements supplied by nature are sun, wind, rain, soil, frost and time. With care and management they can be used to benefit roses.

Sun

The positive purpose of the sun is to provide the energy source for the plant to manufacture food from nutrients and water extracted from the soil. In theory all roses need sunlight for this process. In practice there are some roses that will grow in areas with very little direct sunlight but the site must still have indirect light.

The intensity of sunlight is largely a function of latitude: the farther south, the more intense the sunlight. Farther north the intensity of the sunlight is less, but the hours of sunlight increase during the summer, so what is lost in intensity is partially recovered in longer hours. Very hot, intense sunlight can have a negative effect. In some varieties it will cause scorching of young foliage or even of the flowers (darker colors are more prone to this as they absorb more

Below: Roses excel in a more formal planting, creating a stunning impact with blocks of color.

heat.) Think about your local climate and in areas with intense sunlight, plant to give the roses a little shade in the middle of the day to protect them from the hottest sun. In cool, northern regions try to plant where the rose can exploit longer hours of sunlight. Doing this will give the rose the best chance to please you.

Wind

Several aspects of wind will affect the way your roses grow. We will split them into summer and winter winds.

SUMMER WINDS

Most places will have a prevailing wind, either warm or cold. Warm summer winds will not cause a lot of damage to rose plants. The exception to this is in hot areas. Hot, dry winds will dehydrate plants. Counteract this by planting in the lee of the wind and providing irrigation. If the summer wind is cold this can cause more problems. The worst is encouraging diseases by providing an environment where there can be large rapid fluctuations in temperature. Downy mildew thrives in these conditions. The remedy lies in your choice of resistant varieties and in selecting a site that offers protection from the worst of the prevailing winds. Regular strong cold wind in cooler and exposed regions may also mean the overall height of the plant will be reduced.

Both summer and winter winds are able to cause physical damage. As the rose stems, known as canes, wave in the wind, they will rub together causing abrasions. These are no different than a cut or graze on your arm. An open wound provides easy access for bacteria or disease to attack. In sites that have regular strong winds, shorter plants are better than taller ones.

WINTER WINDS

Winter winds can also cause physical damage. If the plant is tall, a strong wind will rock it in the soil, making the roots loose and reducing their ability to feed the plant. This is made worse in regions where the soil has remained moist during the winter. The cure is simple: give the plant an early winter prune to reduce the area that can catch the wind.

In cold areas winter winds can be very damaging. When the plant is not protected from winter wind it will suffer from the colder temperature caused by the windchill factor. This can freeze the fluids in the stem, rupturing the vessels that carry food and water. These will not repair themselves so the damage is permanent. It is essential to choose hardy varieties and to protect them from cold winds.

Rain

Roses like plenty of moisture – without water there is no life. If you are in a dry area, water plants to make up for the lack of natural rainfall. Irrigation is best done in the morning. Watering in the evening means the area around the rose can remain humid overnight, which encourages the onset of downy mildew. Avoid watering overhead as wet leaves will also encourage mildew. In an area where you have to irrigate because it is hot and there is not enough natural rainfall, plants will often grow taller than normal – if you supply enough water. Too much rain in a soil that retains moisture means damage from

Right: Some roses suffer damage from rain, the petals are bruised and in some cases the flower may never open.

excess rain will occur if the roses stand in a waterlogged area. The roots will begin to rot and die. Plant elsewhere or improve the drainage.

Soil

The soil is vital to a rose. It has the same importance as the foundation has to a building. Without good soil to support growth you can't have a top-quality plant.

Roses like good, fertile soil with lots of decayed organic material in the form of composted manure or vegetation. They like plenty of moisture but do not like to be standing in water. Adding organic material will help roses in any soil. In light, free-draining soils, adding materials helps the soil retain more water. In heavy, wet soils, adding material improves drainage.

Roses are highly adaptable. They thrive in a wide range of different soils. Add lime to increase the pH (alkaline value) of very acidic soil. Adding organic material will help to reduce the pH value of very alkaline soil. You may need to add iron to alkaline soils to keep the plants happy.

There is no substitute for working the soil before planting. The rose will develop a deep root system and its roots need to penetrate the soil easily. Dig the soil well: the deeper you dig the better – but don't bury yourself. Remember that the soil is the foundation to hold the plant up and the refrigerator to store all its food. The only time you can make improvements to the soil is before you plant. Digging the soil well improves the structure, allowing easier penetration for the roots; adding compost, manure or other plant foods will stock up its reserves of food, giving the rose a better start in life.

Frost

There are three stages in the plant's annual cycle when frost can have a damaging effect.

The first is the late spring frost. The plants were pruned in early spring and they have produced fast-growing lush red shoots. These are full of moisture and potential and may be anything from 2 to 10 in (5 to 25 cm) long. The shoots are very vulnerable to frost damage. The very moisture that promotes rapid growth may also prove to be the shoots' downfall. When the spring frost is severe enough to freeze young shoots, they will never fully recover. The moisture turns to ice, and as it does so, it expands, bursting the tube that carries the moisture. That tube will never again carry food or water for the plant.

A frost might damage only 10 percent of the tubes in the stem, or it may damage 80 percent. After light damage the stem will continue to grow until one day the plant needs all the food and water it can muster. The day that the flowers open puts maximum demand on the supply of food and water, and suddenly there is a shortage. The flowers wither and die without ever showing us their beauty.

If the damage is severe the whole stem may wither away without warning on a hot summer day. The damaged stem can never recover; it will only become weaker. Having to support a weak stem is like having a parasite; it is taking from the plant and not contributing.

After a spring frost you need to be able to recognize the extent of the damage. The general guide is that if all the leaves at the top of the stem go limp and hang forlornly, then the damage is serious and you should cut the stem back to allow another unaffected stem to grow and replace it. The other visual effect is that the edges and tips of the leaves discolor, eventually turning brown and crispy. As a rule, this means just the edges of the leaves have suffered and that will not cause any long-term problems. The best remedial action is to acknowledge that you are in an area that has late spring frost and adjust the timing of your spring pruning accordingly. If you prune later the plants may be less prone to this type of damage. Try to avoid getting swept into the mindset that modern consumerism and retailing promote, that "now" or "early" is best. Instead think of nature's calendar and work in a natural time frame, not one to suit commercial interests.

The second frost is an fall frost. A sudden one can cause damage, especially when the plant is still in bloom and there is plenty of movement of fluids in the plant to support the flowers. The presence of these fluids makes the plant vulnerable. In exactly the same way as very young shoots can be damaged by a late spring frost, a sudden fall frost will affect flowering stems. Just how badly will become visible the following spring when you prune: if the pith in the center of the stem is colored brown, the stem must be cut out. A stem like this will never prosper – you are better off without it.

The final frost is a winter frost. Roses are able to withstand much colder temperatures while dormant, because the amount of fluid in the stems is reduced, and therefore the effect of freezing is reduced. The combination of frost and biting wind is more damaging than cold temperatures on their own. We can protect the plant using netting, straw or other insulating materials. A mulch of bark, manure or other organic material over the crown of the plant will help it through the winter by acting rather like a blanket. Don't be tempted to remove this too soon.

Time

This is our commitment. Roses can be made to perform well without becoming a burden, but recognize that there are some essentials: soil preparation before planting, pruning in spring, and finally, time to relax in the summer and enjoy the fruits of our labor. Don't be unrealistic and expect something for nothing.
If you put in the minimum effort, then accept that results will be reasonable, not perfect.

It is very rare to have all of these natural elements in perfect balance. The trick is to know that where one aspect is weak, then we must be fair to the plant and give it the best chance by providing good conditions in other areas. Compromise is acceptable so long as it is a good compromise. It is only when we give too many poor resources that the plant will respond with a display of truculence and refuse to behave in the way we want it to.

Below: The effect of frost may be pretty, but any soft, young growth will be damaged by it.

Planning and Design

Here we enter one of the most enjoyable areas of gardening. This is our chance to create our own landscape in harmony with nature. You can employ a professional designer, who may provide a wonderful garden design. The alternative is to enjoy the organic evolution of your own garden. As you change the garden over the years and as you incorporate different aspects, the plants and ideas you have will be your own. These ideas will be a reminder of a phase of your life, of a person or a place you visited. A garden is living, developing and evolving all the time. No design is ever complete: there are always changes that you can make to include some new feeling from your life.

Roses can be incorporated in any and every garden. They are just like you and your clothes. Sometimes you go to work in a suit, to give the right impression. On many occasions you are at leisure in shorts and T-shirt. In the evening you might wear evening dress and exude an elegant graceful air. There is a time and place for each different style. Roses are the same. They can be functional, graceful or beautiful; they are certainly versatile and able to blend into formal or informal designs. Some appear to be bashful and shy; others are bold and brash. All have a beauty for us to discover and enjoy. A garden is a place to reflect moods: the rose helps to create these effects.

The first task in design is to select a position that will suit the plants. We have already looked at the factors that will influence how plants perform. To recap in brief: they need a light position with some direct sunlight – they do not want to be overshadowed by trees. As a guide assume that the roots of a mature tree will affect the soil in the entire area under the canopy and another 10 ft (3 m) beyond. It is not just the light that is compromised by the tree: it takes moisture and food from the soil, as well. Good fertile soil is required, not too wet and not too dry. Think about the wind, the frost, other natural aspects. Take this opportunity to design trouble out of your garden

The second task is to decide what size plants you want to grow. This is important and should be done before you start thinking whether you want red, pink or any other color flowers. The ultimate size of the plant will dictate whether it is the right rose for the position you have selected. It is virtually impossible to reduce the size of a rose plant. If, with good pruning the plant grows to 4 ft (1.2 m) tall, then that is its size. It is possible to let it grow taller with lighter

Below: Using a rampant climber or rambler to cover a small building is informal and very effective.

Above: The colors blend beautifully together in this informal planting.

pruning, but it is not possible to reduce the size without some undesirable side effect, such as constant summer pruning, which will reduce the amount of bloom the plant can produce.

Ascertaining the size of a plant is difficult. Different books and catalogues often credit one rose with a range of ultimate heights. To plan our garden we need to understand how commercial growers accredit the heights to varieties, and how our garden's microclimate and growing conditions will affect height. Remember that it is best to work with nature.

As a rule a nursery will give the minimum height that you can expect a rose variety to attain. This is a logical starting point, given the fundamental rule that you can let it get taller. Factors that will influence the size of the plant in your garden are:

Soil A rich, fertile soil will grow a stronger and taller plant. A light, poor soil will grow a weaker and smaller plant.

Sun In a region that is sunny with warm weather early in the year, more growth will be produced (provided there is enough water), giving a bigger plant.

Wind In a windy position the plant will react by remaining shorter, especially in cold wind.

Rain Without enough rain in the growing season the plant will remain small. With a combination of sun, heat and water all together, the plant will become large.

The third task is to walk into the garden and plan the area that we want to plant. It is two

Below: Example of a rough planting plan. The plants in the front should all be slightly shorter than those behind them; colors are arranged in a symmetrical pattern left to right; based on viewing from either end or the front.

Short	Medium		Tall		Medium	Short
			Rear of the bed			
x x 3 "Betty Boop"	x x 2 "Easy Going"	x	x x 2 "Mountbatten"	x	x x 2 "Easy Going"	x x 3 "Betty Boop"
x x 1 "Princess of Wales"	x x 2 "Aimant"	x 1 "Amber Abundance"	x x 4 "Betty Harkness"	x 1 "Amber Abundance"	x x 2 "IAimant"	x x 1 "Princess of Wales"

Above: The formal walkway is a visual treat as well as enthralling for the sense of smell.

dimensional on the ground but we have to also incorporate for the third dimension – the height of the plants. We can get shape into our roses by adjusting the length and breadth of the area we are planting. We can have an area that is any shape, a square, rectangle, circle or random curves. We can also get shape into our roses by using the different heights of the plants. Effects can be introduced, such as undulations to give the impression of waves, graduation from shortest to tallest, or sudden peaks of height.

The fourth task is to jot a rough plan on paper. It need not be to scale, but it should have the rough shape of the area, with dimensions written down. It always helps to show where north is, because then we can assess the light, sunrise and sunset. Next draw in any prominent features: big trees that will affect light and soil; paths; your house; unsightly eyesores that you want to block out; any slope to the site. Add a couple of arrows showing your prime viewing directions. How will it look from my patio, my window, my entrance gate? Do I need a tall plant to block a view of the compost area? Now is the time to ask questions.

The fifth task is to decide what style we want reflected in our garden. Some roses are light, airy, graceful and elegant. Others will be strong, bold, almost heavy. Do you want a definite statement using an intense splash of color or a subtle complement to other aspects of the garden? Are you mixing colors or planting in groups of the same variety? There are many questions of style, fashion and individual choice. The last is the important one: remember who the garden is for and who it should please most. Do it in your own individual way and enjoy your own interaction with nature.

Task number six is to start thinking about a planting plan. By now you know the shape and size of the area for planting, the size of the plants that you want, the style that you wish to express. The only remaining jobs are the planting plan and the colors. To draw a planting plan you need to use a reasonably accurate scale. Decide on the planting distance that you want to use (2½ ft/0.75 m apart is a good average) and mark the planting positions on the plan. Either plant in rows, as in a matrix, or in staggered rows.

Make a list of those varieties you want to include, the "must have" list. The second list is "I like it but I can live without it." If you are planting in groups now is the time to divide the plants up. Three of a kind is usually the minimum; five give a dash of color; whereas seven and upwards give a splash of color. Try to use groups of different sizes. If all the roses are planted in the same number – all threes or all fives – they will look regimented and lack vitality and inspiration.

It is always a good policy to select the tallest varieties first. The main reason for this is that there are fewer tall varieties than short ones, so it is wise to build the design round the available tall varieties. It is now a process of personal choice. Selecting colors that contrast or graduate gently in tone is one way. Or consider random use of color, or use of colors all within one range, say pinks and reds, or orange to yellow. Or use the colors to create symmetry or a pattern. Find pictures of the roses and place cutouts on your plan to give an idea of the color selections you have made.

The traditionalist will argue that roses should be grown alone. I disagree. Roses are unusual as garden plants in that they make a wonderful display on their own. There are very few species that have the array of attributes found in every rose garden. But because of its ability and success to make its own garden, the rose has suffered from an ill-informed view that it is a loner, that it only likes its own company. How wrong that is. My suggestion is that it's a great mixer. It can add color, shape or perfume to a multitude of garden situations. Climbing roses can be grown in tandem with clematis, increasing both the flowering time and the color range available. Mixed shrub borders benefit from the intensity of a flowering rose and the perfume and flowering time. Ground-cover roses provide brilliant displays in patio tubs and even in hanging baskets. There is no position that is forbidden if you keep an open mind.

Right: Many cities have excellent public rose gardens, great places to see a range of varieties.

How to Choose

Knowing how to choose the plants you want will make everything easier. In some respects it is like decorating your home. In the kitchen you will be looking for colors that suit the activities, plus a floor covering that will withstand wear and tear. A bedroom will require a different approach: there may be softer colors, there may be lace, there may be more romance.

New or old varieties

Both new and old varieties can be beautiful. There are good new varieties and others that are not so good. The same applies to old varieties. To help you decide, the development of the car provides a useful analogy. Today you can buy a new car, it is reliable and, if it goes wrong, the garage can fix it easily. Use it every day, pay it virtually no attention, it has all mod cons and performs very well. Alternatively you can buy an old car. There are a few that retain reliability and can be used every day. Many require additional time, attention and care. They are a hobby, not for everyday use. They do not have all mod cons, are slower, less refined and comfortable. If you want an easy-care garden with modern standards of performance, then focus mainly on newer varieties. If you have time and want a rewarding and absorbing hobby, then start a collection of both new and old.

The properties that modern roses have in abundance over many of the older varieties are found in the following areas. (table below)

Overall newer varieties will provide the easiest route to a colorful and easy-to-care for display. Just remember the improvements in features, performance and comfort of cars over the past 100 years. Roses have improved in a similar way.

Varieties that suit your microclimate

Roses respond to local conditions in different ways. You should assess the following:

Are the varieties hardy in my area?	Pick only ones that are hardy enough
Do I live in an area of intense sunlight?	Avoid varieties that fade or discolor in intense sunlight
Is my garden in an area that will suffer heavy rain during the flowering period?	Disregard varieties with flowers that suffer in wet conditions
Will they be in a very windy position?	Don't go for varieties that are too tall or have very large heavy flowers.

Constitution	The modern bush will have stronger stems and make more new stems from the base, giving a sturdy strong plant. Varieties tend to be more vigorous than older varieties. They combine vigor with plants that do not become too tall.
Foliage	Many modern varieties have leaves that are placed more closely along the stem. This makes the plant look more lush.
Flower	Modern varieties produce a larger number of flowers in a flush, and very often they will repeat bloom more quickly. For the amount of color provided they are streets ahead of most older varieties.
Health	Many modern varieties will be healthier than their older counterparts. Health is something that can never be guaranteed. It is subject to the physiological state of the plant. If the plant is under stress it is prone to become diseased. If it is growing without stress, its natural resistance will increase. Modern varieties tend to have greater resistance than the older ones.
Scent	There are very few differences between modern and old. For both categories there are a range: some are strongly scented, some have no scent, and most are in between. It is an ill-informed myth that modern roses have no scent. Some roses have scent and some don't. That has always been a truism.

Above: Modern varieties not only produce more flower than older varieties, but have more dense and attractive foliage than old varieties. The leaf is important – we look at it when the plant is not in flower!

Varieties that are the right size

As already stated in the Planning and Design section, this is fundamental if you want your roses to look right. A tall plant growing where a short one is needed (or vice versa) will look wrong and it will always annoy you, until you move it.

The style

Formal, informal, modern, cottage, hybrid tea, floribunda, shrub – there are numerous options. Do not be afraid to mix plants that others consider to come from divergent categories. The selection should reflect what you like, not what others ordain as acceptable. As in home decoration, one person's taste may be the antithesis of another's. Both are right, neither is wrong. What is right is for individuals to express their own taste in their own space.

Color

I always leave the selection of color until last. I know that you will have decided early in the process that your ultimate desire is a ruby red rose, for example. However, there is no point in looking at ruby red roses until you have established which type is suitable.

Based on this information, select varieties that suit you and will perform just as you want them to. You can add criteria that are important to you: health and scent are obvious candidates. The selection process may well end up with a degree of compromise. We are dealing with nature and frequently you will find that nature cannot provide you with exactly what you want. You may have to give on color in order to get the size you want, but that is choice – making your own decisions on the priority of the various elements that create the whole.

It is much better to look for something knowing what you want. If you start looking for a red rose, you will find a vast array. Most of them will be unsuitable for some reason or another. The tighter your specification before you begin to look, the more successful you will be at achieving your goals.

	Questions	Sample answers
1	Modern or old?	Modern variety preferred
2	Suit my microclimate?	Can cope with strong sunlight
3	What size do I want?	Grows 3 ft (1 m) tall
4	The style?	Hybrid tea or floribunda
5	Color?	Ruby red.

How to Buy

Roses are a part of our leisure and pleasure. And there is no reason why buying them should not be a pleasure, too. It is not like doing essential household shopping. This is a part of the wider experience of planning, design and enjoyment.

Rose varieties are on sale through a range of outlets. It is personal choice how you wish to buy, although it is sometimes influenced by family and friends. My comments are only a guide.

Rose specialist catalogues/ general nurseries

Many specialist growers produce catalogues. Some are illustrated, some rely on words. This is the route to the maximum choice of varieties. Do remember that they are catalogues and, as such, should be read as if they are the words of a salesperson. The quality of service and plants will vary. Some are excellent, some barely acceptable.

Garden centers

These are easy and convenient – most people live close to a garden center. Many centers keep roses in stock for most of the year, catering for the "instant" effect prevalent in so much modern retailing and advertising. Some garden centers provide a limited range of roses, and some a good range. The standard of rose care is usually lower than if you visit a specialist.

Garden shows

Horticultural shows and exhibitions are great venues for ideas; for seeing what is new, what is available in the marketplace, finding new suppliers and researching the product. My personal advice would be do not order at a show unless you planned to do so before you left home. Everything is different at a show. The exhibits are staged and manicured, and not at all natural. Exhibitors offer incentives to buy, and to their staff to sell. It can be a more pressurized purchase. You can lose track of scale: everything at an exhibition is big or oversized, which warps your mind's view of your scale at home.

Municipal or specialist gardens

Visiting gardens is a great way to investigate varieties. In most you will see how they grow and perform. In many you will also see how the variety looks not only at its best, but also at its worst. This is vital: roses all look good at their best, but some age gracefully, others disgracefully.

Internet

The Internet is a great way to see a lot of roses. Most of the specialist nurseries have Web sites, many with online ordering. In addition to the specialists there are general gardening sites that sell some roses. The pros and cons are similar to those for specialist nurseries and garden centers.

Special offers

These are always very tempting, but you are buying what someone else wants to sell to you, not what you want. Take advantage if they suit you. If they are not what you want, leave them alone.

Nostalgia

A route that can provide us with enjoyment or disappointment. On the down side, our memories are not as accurate as we would like to believe. Frequently we can visualize the perfection of our grandparents' garden, that beautiful rose that was always in flower, with its wonderful perfume. How we'd love to try to recreate that ideal. Alas, it is rarely as we remember. The passage of time has corrupted our minds: the rose was not really in flower all the time, the scent we recollect is the one we would like it to have been. We remember the ideal, not the reality. We trace the variety only to find it lets us down in our garden.

Friends' recommendations

Recent experience is better than vague memories. If you share the same objectives as a friend then this can work. If your friend spends more time on his roses than you are going to, then your results may not be so good. If your friend is competitive and you are not, then do not get drawn in to comparisons. Try to create your own identity and just use what you see to be the best of your friend's varieties or ideas.

What to expect

There is one important aspect to remember: our roses are a hobby, we are growing them for pleasure. A part of our enjoyment should be the purchase of the plants. If you enjoy shopping for your plants and take time to find the varieties you want and high-quality plants, it will be a big step towards overall satisfaction.

We should also understand what to expect when we buy roses. Shopping at garden centers is pretty straightforward: we look at the available plants, select the ones we want and take them home. Ordering from the Internet or a rose-grower's mail-order catalogue is different. As the consumer you need to be sure that you understand all the details. The important issue is, when will the plants be delivered? Traditionally this is during the dormant (fall/winter/spring) period, when roses are despatched as bare-root plants. This means the roots are bare, the plants are dug from the field and sent to you without any soil around them. If you order in summer your roses won't be delivered until fall, and the plants will flower the following summer. However, if you order in winter, delivery will be almost immediate. The other alternative which is becoming more widespread, is for Internet and specialist growers to despatch potted plants in season. This allows you to order in summer and receive the plants within a few days, making the service almost as quick as going to the local garden center.

When your plants arrive is important. Before you purchase or receive delivery there are a few basic tasks you should have completed. Have you planned where the plants will go? Have you checked that the natural conditions are suitable? Have you dug and fed the area to be planted? Have you removed any weeds that were growing there? Only when you can answer "Yes" to these questions are you ready for the plants. The last thing you want to do is to have them hanging around while you do the preparation. If they arrive before you are ready to plant you will rush the preparation and take shortcuts, which will have a detrimental effect on your roses. Be prepared – it makes it all a pleasure instead of a rush.

Below: It is important to buy good plants. The plant on the left has had too many roots cut off, and the one on the right looks as if it was stuffed (instead of potted) into a pot that is too small. It should not be sticking out of the pot like this.

The Growing Cycle

In this section we will look at the life of a rose, covering the jobs you should do and the jobs you have to do. We will start with planting, the beginning of the life cycle.

Bare-root roses

Bare root is the traditional way of planting and in many ways is still the best way. Here are some rules to observe.

CHECK THE QUALITY BEFORE PLANTING

Plants need a good root system and an adequate quantity of stems. They need to be free from material damage and free from obvious signs of disease. Let's start with the root system. If there is just one tap root, that's not good. It's best if the root divides and branches out. What we need is plenty of fine root, not a little coarse root. Two strong stems is all right, though not ideal; three or more is best.

CARE BEFORE PLANTING

It is very important to look after the plants between the time you get them and the time you plant them. Bare-root plants are very resilient. They can withstand storage, transport and all manner of treatment that you would imagine to be damaging. Just think of where they would be in the natural world. Bare-root plants come in winter when they are dormant. Under natural conditions they would be outside, where it would be cold and frosty. That tells us how to keep them until we plant them: keep them cold, also out of direct sunlight and moist. They can be wrapped in wet newspaper and sealed in polyethylene bags and left somewhere cold (within five degrees of freezing) for at least three weeks. As soon as they begin to dry out they will begin to die. The two elements that cause drying out are heat and air circulation. While it is best to plant as soon as you can, if you have to store plants these are the conditions to do it in. Just check they are still moist and reseal the bag.

Below: When buying bare root roses, select those whose roots have not been chopped too short.

PLANTING TIME FOR BARE-ROOT ROSES

They can be planted at any time in fall and spring (and in some regions, also the winter) when the ground is not severely frozen. If there is a frost overnight which clears by midday, then carry on and plant.

PLANTING METHOD

Roses are easy to plant. All you need is reasonable conditions. Prepare the site by digging it over, removing weeds and adding some organic material (manure or compost). With the planting location prepared, all you have to do is dig a hole large enough to accommodate the roots of the plant. It can be a round, square, any old shaped hole. Make it deep enough – 10 to 12 in (25 to 30 cm) is plenty. Put the plant into the hole. If you have to bend the roots a bit, that is fine, and trimming an inch (2.5 cm) off the ends of them is helpful.

When the plant is sitting in the hole add a generous amount of compost. This will supply food and a good soil texture for the first new roots to penetrate. Wobble and shake the plant so that the compost falls between the roots. Replace half the soil, which should be crumbly. Hold the stem of the plant with one hand to keep it at the right depth, then use your feet to tread the soil down to ensure the plant is firm. Add the rest of the soil and tramp down on the surface again, using all your weight.

The only other point is to establish the planting depth. And that will depend on nature.

1 *Dig a hole that is big enough. Don't worry if you bend the roots a little.*

2 *Put some good compost around the roots to help the rose get established.*

3 *When the hole is half- to three-quarters full of soil, firm the soil with your foot.*

4 *Fill the hole and trample down with your foot, making sure the planting is at the correct depth. Water well.*

Above: A potted climbing plant in early spring with healthy new growth starting.

Above: The root system holds the soil together. Young white roots can be seen. Note – the plant is not pot bound (where the roots go round and round.)

The point of reference is the "crown" of the plant, where the rose you have chosen is grafted onto the host root by the nursery.

The first variable provided by nature is your soil type. Is it a dry soil – or is it a soil that retains moisture and is wet? In dry conditions it is OK to plant the crown up to 2 in (5 cm) below the soil level. In wet soils keep the crown just above soil level. If you plant too deeply in wet soils, the buried stems will begin to rot. In average soil plant with the crown at ground level.

The second aspect of nature that will change the way you plant is if you are in an area that has extremely cold winters. In many regions of North America the crown would have to be planted 2 to 4 in (5 to 10 cm) below soil level to help ensure the plant's survival through the winter. You will also need to protect the crown of the plant over winter. This can be with a deep mound of straw, soil or other insulating material.

When the rose is happily planted there is one more task, water it in. At least 1 gallon (4.55 litres) of water per plant, please. If conditions are dry and windy, water every couple of days until spring.

CARE AFTER PLANTING BARE-ROOT ROSES

If the planting is carried out in good soil, very little immediate after care is required. Keep moist is the mantra that you must follow (see also Pruning on page 34).

Problems with bare-root roses

There are no real problems in planting bare-root roses, only disbelief that a plant in such a naked and unprotected state will grow and thrive. Because the plant has no soil and no protection, there is an assumption that it will be weak and vulnerable. However, provided the plants are kept in the right conditions prior to planting and are protected properly from very cold, wet or windy conditions, they should survive. Both you and the nursery that supplies the plant must keep the plants in good condition. Choose a good nursery that excels in plant quality, packaging and delivery, if purchasing by mail order. When bare-root roses are planted firmly and kept moist, then this is the easiest and best way of planting with a success rate of well over 90 percent.

Potted, pot-grown or containerized roses

CHECK THE QUALITY BEFORE PLANTING

First I will explain what a potted, pot-grown or containerized rose is. It is simply a bareroot rose that a nursery has dug out of the field and placed in a pot. It is as simple as that. The only reason for doing this is to satisfy consumer demand by extending the planting season beyond the colder months.

To check that you are buying good plants look at the plant and its foliage, the pot it is in and the soil.

Do the plants look happy, with clean green leaves? Are they nice and bushy with strong stems? Are they new stock or left over from last year?

If you see any of the following, don't buy the plant: diseases such as downy mildew, powdery mildew, blackspot and rust (see the information on pp 28–33). If a garden center is selling plants with these ailments, go elsewhere. Also look out for insects such as caterpillars and aphids. If there are only a few on a plant, that is probably all right. If there are a lot, go elsewhere to purchase, or point out the problem and tell the garden center you will return in a few days, by which time the problem should have been sorted out.

Yellowing upper leaves can be a sign that the plant is undernourished. Roses should not have a yellow tinge to the foliage.

If the lower leaves are yellowing there are three possible reasons. The plants may be over watered or packed too closely together so that insufficient light gets to the foliage at the base. Roses can recover from of either of these. The third reason is if the plant has blackspot or downy mildew – both of these form spots on the leaf, which will lose all its green color and turn yellow. If the leaves are yellow with dark spots of discoloration, don't buy the plant.

Moss or algae growing on the oldest stems at the base of the plant could indicate old stock. The plant could be pot bound, where the roots become too confined to the pot and go around in tight circles.

Next look at the pot. Is it big enough to support the plant? It should be a reservoir of food and water and not so small that it cramps the roots too much.

Make sure the pots aren't so small that most of the root has been cut off to get the plant into the pot.

Any container less than a gallon is on the small side, but it may be adequate for less mature shrubs and will sustain a plant into early summer. However, when the plant begins to flower and demand higher levels of food and water, its development will be inhibited.

A container of 1 gallon is the smallest pot that will sustain a rose plant in good condition. If the garden center has a correct regime of maintenance, then this size is acceptable.

Larger pots offer more scope and potential for the plant to grow and develop without stress; pots for roses can go up to 3 gallons in size.

Finally, check the soil. It is the foundation of the plant, so it has to be good. If it dries out too quickly that will cause you difficulties in your garden. Does it contain it a slow-release fertilizer to carry on feeding the plant? Is it free of weeds? Do not be afraid to ask the sales assistant to take a plant out of its pot. You will soon see whether it is well watered and if there is good root development.

As with bare-root roses, it is advisable to do the planting preparation before you buy the plants. However, if you have to keep the plants in pots for a while before planting you must look after them. They will have come from a garden center where plants are watered on a regular basis – for most of the spring and summer periods at least once a day. If you suddenly change its routine the plant will be upset. Keep plants well watered on a daily basis.

PLANTING TIME

Potted plants can be planted in the spring, summer and fall. If it is very hot and dry that can also stress the plants – water them well.

PLANTING METHOD

Assuming the soil is prepared and in good condition, then planting is easy. Start by giving the pot a good soaking. Dig a hole that is a little larger than the pot. Make sure the soil at the base of the hole is friable or crumbly and then add a little compost. Remove the plant from the pot and place carefully in the hole; place earth around it, using a mixture of soil and compost. Tread in firmly on all sides and water well. The planting depth is the same for both pot-grown roses and bare-root ones.

CARE AFTER PLANTING POT-GROWN ROSES

These require more care than bare-root roses they are to become established quickly and successfully. Remember that where the soil acts in the same way to a plant as the foundations do to a building. By taking a plant from a pot we are bound to disturb the soil around the delicate root structure, and placing it into different soil can be a cultural shock – like picking a building up from a city and placing it in a wilderness. To counter this shock is very simple: water. If the ambient conditions are dry then water on a regular basis for the first four weeks. (And remember the plant was accustomed to daily watering in the garden center.) In the medium term, check that there is no settling of the soil that the plant was grown in. In some instances it will dry out and shrink, but the soil in the garden will not shrink. When this happens a gap develops between the original root ball of the plant and the garden soil. Water will not travel between the two properly and the plant will dry out and die. Fill any gap with soil and water well.

THE RISKS OF PLANTING POT-GROWN ROSES

If the right amount of water is administered, then planting potted roses is successful. You should achieve close to 100 percent success. If the plants are poor, or they have suffered before planting then success rates will plummet to about 66 percent.

Ongoing rose care

I will leave pruning until the next section of the book and start with early and mid-season care. This is the period that starts after pruning and finishes as the first flowers begin to open.

Good news here: there is very little to do. If you have done the preparation and planting well, the plants will be largely self-managing. However, we still have to pay attention to them and respond to the conditions that nature provides. We can take action to improve results. On page 15 we looked at how to deal with winter frosts by using mulches. They may also be used to keep plant roots cool and moist, and can be effective at keeping weeds down. Roses like lots of food. Add fertilizer to boost growth prior to flowering.

MOISTURE

If there is a dry spell, then water. I always advise watering early in the day if possible. Evening watering allows greater nighttime humidity, which can lead to disease.

FROST

Where late frosts damage the lush new shoots of spring, treat them as described on p 14. See also information on protective mulching on p 15.

WIND

If the wind is violent it can cause damage by making branches rub together or by snapping young shoots. Cut out the damage to protect against disease.

Diseases affecting foliage

Be vigilant and spot early signs of trouble. There is a range of fungi whose spores travel on the wind and spread diseases liable to attack roses. They are listed and described here in their likely order of appearance during the season.

DOWNY MILDEW

It likes conditions where air circulation is poor. It likes humidity, warm days and cold nights.It tends to attack young foliage, creating irregular marks on the leaves. These are extremely dark, but when held up to the light, they have a slightly purple hue. As the fungus grows the leaf turns yellow before it falls from the plant. Downy mildew is most common before the flowers open. The cures lie in the resistance of the variety you chose to plant, and secondly in growing the plant well so that it is stress free and has maximum natural resistance. Good ventilation and humidity help, as does the application of an effective fungicide.

POWDERY MILDEW

This is often the most noticeable of the fungal diseases, but in many ways the least damaging. Unsightly, yes, but not threatening to the life of the plant, it is the common white powdery substance that appears very often on young growth in the second half of the season. It is more prevalent in hot, dry summers. Either put up with it or use a treatment from a garden center.

BLACKSPOT

This disease attacks older leaves, but will not normally be seen until after the first flush of flowers is over. Keep an eye on the lower leaves. As its name tells you, it will appear as black spots on the leaf. In appearance it is similar to downy mildew, except it tends to form on older foliage first. The spots are black and close to a perfect circle in shape. In time the leaf will turn yellow and fall prematurely.

There is a common thread running through the management of these diseases – think about nature. The first and best defence against disease is to have a plant that is growing with vigor. The plant is just like you and I: under stress we are more susceptible to illness and so are plants. There are many natural occurrences that will trigger stress, including poor soil, drought, uneven watering, waterlogging, poor light, poor feeding and finally exhaustion. You may consider this last factor a strange concept for plants, but it happens where a plant has produced a mass of flowers. Flowering uses a lot of energy, food and water. Remember that the objective of all plants and animals is to breed. The flower is no more than an exotic display to attract the bees that do the

Below: An example of powdery mildew, which looks like white powder on the leaves.

pollination to further the species. We all know the effort teenagers put into looking just right, and how tired they are after a week of discos and parties. Roses are the same after flowering, so give them a boost. Feed them just before they come into flower (remember it takes time for the fertilizer to get down to the roots), so that they benefit and recover quickly from the effort of flowering.

RUST

Most modern roses have a strong resistance to rust. It is another fungus whose spores travel by air. The first sign will be pustules two or three times the size of a pinhead on the undersides of the leaves. These give the fungus its name – they are rust colored, turning black with time. It tends to attack leaves on the lower part of the plant. But its presence will be noticeable from the upper leaf as the veins in the leaf turn yellow.

The leaf will fall off after a severe attack. This is another fungus that enjoys damp conditions. Damage is caused not only to the leaf, but to the stem where the leaf joins it. and it can prevent the auxiliary bud from that leaf node developing into a strong shoot in the future. There are products for preventing the spread of rust.

Controlling disease

Disease management can be set up by providing good soil, site and planting. The next method is to observe the plants. If one plant is susceptible to disease every year, it will always be the first to suffer and spread the disease. There is a good argument for removing that particular plant. This is little more than natural selection: in nature the weakest of the species will perish. Why not copy nature in the garden? To me it seems like a successful, if sometimes ruthless, model to follow.

At this stage we reach one of the points at which different gardeners will proceed in different directions. The choices are to accept a small level of disease and do nothing, attempt to reduce any disease with organic methods or to try to control disease with fungicides.

I have to say that in principle it is bad gardening practice to grow diseased plants in the garden, as there can be a build up over a number of years, making control harder and harder. On the other hand in a leisure/pleasure garden I do not believe that it is essential to control disease completely. In the most natural sense there is a place on earth for both the plant and the disease that is a parasite on it.

In gardening terms, the analogy I use to imagine a plant under stress should work both ways. Is it worth the human stress of trying to keep the plants in a perfect condition? To do so requires a dedication that goes beyond leisure and can become pressure. When a hobby becomes a pressure it will cease to be so much of a pleasure. It is natural for a parasite and its host to cohabit, so my personal position is that a

Left: Blackspot – this fungus makes round black marks on the leaves, which will then turn yellow and fall off.

low level of managed disease is acceptable in the leisure garden.

There are numerous organic potions that can help to keep plants healthy, with new ones arriving on a regular basis. Try them if you like the sound of them. The chemical fungicide market is in constant turmoil with new additions and deletions to the range. Use chemicals to control severe outbreaks and to stop the spread of the disease.

Insect damage

The next area of control is to limit the damage caused by insects. This again has to be taken to the level that you are content with. To keep all insects away all of the time is a tough task. Better to accept that there are insects about and just try to limit any overly serious attacks. The worst insects are described here.

APHIDS

Aphids commonly visit roses. The damage from these occurs as they suck a sugar solution from the plant. As they are greedy little devils they keep sucking the plant's sugars out even when they have had enough, so it passes through them and becomes a sticky mess on the leaves and around the flower bud.

This causes two problems. The aphids are eating the food that the plant has made for itself, while the sticky sugary deposits are an easy surface for a fungus to stick to and gain an initial foothold to infest the plant. Aphids multiply very quickly. Having an unusual lifestyle, in which the male is not required for reproduction, they breed at an astounding rate. A large colony will make a mess of a plant: it becomes unattractive and sticky to touch.

There are many forms of control, all of which will work to some degree. It is worth experimenting with planting companion plants such as African marigolds, which aphids find unattractive. Although aphids blow around on the wind, they have enough flight control to decide whether to visit your garden or one half a mile down the road. Prevention has to be worth a try.

The second method is to encourage biological control. Other insects and some birds feed on aphids. Ladybugs are particularly keen on them, so encourage more beneficial insects into your garden. Thirdly you can purchase a biological control – a predator that will live on your plants and consume the aphids for you. Then there is spraying. A weak solution of dishwashing liquid with water can help – it breaks down the surface tension of the water, which will then form a film rather than individual droplets, and this film of water will suffocate the aphids. The alternative is to use one of the many commercial insecticides.

RED SPIDER MITE

This is a destructive little critter. The individual mites are tiny, best seen through a magnifying

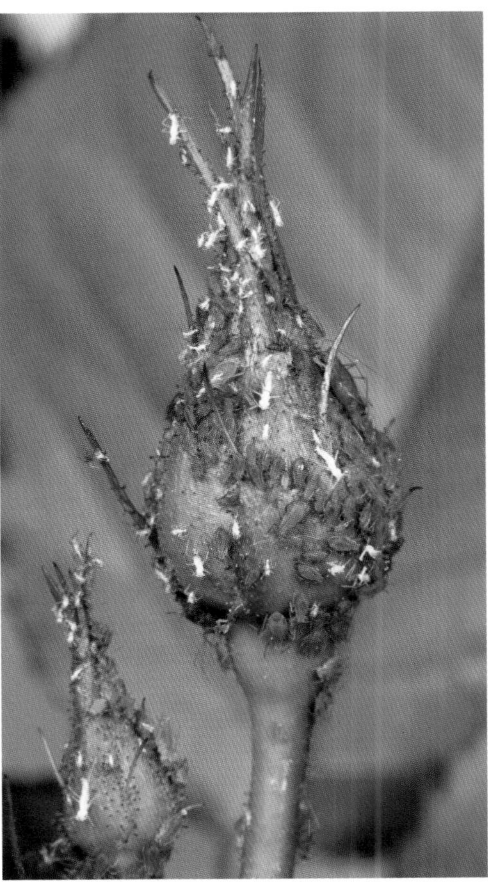

Right: Aphids – commonly called greenfly. They suck the sugary sap from the plant making the flower bud and stem sticky.

glass. They lay thousands of eggs on the underside of the leaf, and the eggs are more visible than the adults. The leaf takes on a bronzed sickly hue. Red spider mites will appear in warm, dry spots. They love plants against a wall and plants with very dense, small leaves, but will also go for plants with big leaves. They make the plant look sick, starting with leaves low down and working their way upwards. Red spider mites hate water, and fairly high-pressure squirts of water on the underside of the leaf will slow progress. The best control is biological, using a predator to eat them up.

WESTERN FLOWER THRIP

As the name indicates, thrips are interested in flowers. Thrips are tiny – the next size up from the thunder fly and much smaller than aphids. They get into the flower buds and chew the petals. As the flowers open all the petals will have a disfigured brown edge, be shortened and generally look a mess. They prefer warm climates and are becoming more common in the UK. Use biological predators or chemical control.

POLLEN BEETLE

These are harmless to the plant but unpleasant to us. The small black beetles are an agricultural pest and like to live on the yellow flowers of canola. However, that crop stops flowering just before roses bloom, when the pollen beetle looks for another home. Roses are one of the subjects they choose, especially the yellows, whites and some orange shades. Just look before you sniff, unless you enjoy beetles up your nose.

CATERPILLARS

The young of moths and butterflies will munch away at rose leaves and can leave the foliage in tatters. I never like destroying all caterpillars, as some grow into magnificent and beautiful adult butterflies. Nature offers a partial cure as birds will eat some; chemical control will stop them ruining your plants completely.

SAWFLY

The leaf-rolling sawfly is adept at winding up rose growers. The adults live in trees – part of a copse or woodland – and rarely in gardens. Adult flies visit rose bushes to lay eggs on the leaves. The female poisons each leaf that she lays an egg on, causing it to roll up as neatly as any Havana cigar. By making a tightly rolled tube, the sawfly creates a safe and protected home for its egg, out of sight of predators and protected from the weather. Many leaves on a plant can be infected. Apart from the strange appearance – lots of rolled-up leaves can look as if there is a batch of birds' feet hanging on the plant – it does little harm. The leaf will still work and feed the rose. It is hard to treat, as the instigator of the complaint is just a visitor for a fleeting moment to lay her eggs. Either pick the leaves off or ignore them.

Insect management

With the exception of aphids, which breed without the assistance of a partner, it is often essential to deal with insects twice. A little understanding of an insect's life cycle helps. Adults lay eggs, which go through an adolescent (too-young-to-breed) stage before they mature. If on a given day there are some insects at each stage and you use a treatment, it will be effective on the adults and adolescents. Even if you had 100 percent success, another generation will hatch from the eggs and develop through the adolescent stage to adults in a few days. The second treatment needs to catch those adolescents before they mature and lay another generation of eggs. If you do a little research and find out what you are battling, the battle is far easier to win.

Other pests

Hundreds of different insects may visit your roses. Many of them are harmless, appear only for a few days or do limited damage. Small populations of insects will not do as much harm as animals such as deer or rabbits. These can strip the leaves and bark from the plant. The best long-term protection from this type of wildlife is fencing. Deer are particularly partial to new young shoots in spring. Winter damage can be far worse. When there is only a limited amount of food available, rabbits can strip the bark from the stems of the roses at ground level.

This can only be treated by cutting out the damaged wood. When the bark is stripped, there is an open wound into the life-giving heart of the plant. The wound will become infected and a weak point unless it is removed.

More growing-season tasks

There are two other growing-season tasks. Repeat flowering uses lots of energy, so please feed plants to keep them healthy. The second task is deadheading, which also helps conserve a plant's energy. When a flower has finished blooming the ovary remains, which will turn into a seed pod. The sole objective of a plant is to propagate itself by forming seeds in a seed pod. By deadheading we achieve two results. Stopping the plant from forming a seed pod means the plant thinks, "Hey, no seed, no offspring. I will have to make more flowers to produce another crop of seed." And that is just what we wanted – more flowers. The other benefit of deadheading is also linked to seed production. Producing a seed pod is a bit like a pregnancy – it takes a lot of energy from the mother. If we prevent seed pods from forming after flowering, the plant will put more effort into producing better growth, and more growth means more flowers.

Our final annual task is pruning, the next topic. Most of the actions that you need to take in the growing season are common sense. The better the decisions you make early in the growing process, the less time you will have to spend on dreary maintenance.

Plan the site, give the plants enough space and air, good soil, make a good choice of varieties and then plant well. If you get these prerequisites right, future work is immeasurably reduced. Regular feeding and watering will be your main tasks to assure great results.

Below: This caterpillar has plenty more growing to do before he is mature and he will eat most of these leaves.

Pruning

There is only one statement that I want to make at the start of this section, because I know people think pruning is complicated, difficult and confusing. But in my view it is far better to give it a go and achieve a partial success than not try at all.

In truth pruning is quite easy. Let's start with explaining why we do it. I would like to borrow from nature to help me. Before mankind cultivated roses – indeed, before mankind existed – roses were pruned. Not in an accurate or precise fashion, but by the environment they lived in. As a result of the harsh treatment dished out by nature, roses thrived and spread across the globe. There is a hint in here: harsh treatment works. In nature, pruning could take place in a variety of ways. Frost may have killed off many canes on a plant, grazing animals could cut them down, lightening might start a fire or a large tree felled by the wind could indiscriminately crush the branches of a rose. There are many more ways in which plants could be cut back by nature, but the idea I want to express is that it is the act of cutting back that is important – the precision of the cut is secondary.

1 *A mature bush rose that has had regular pruning in the past.*

What is the point of pruning? It benefits both the plant and the gardener.

For the plant it is all about vigor, vitality, virility. When a plant is young it produces stems full of energy. As a stem ages it becomes similar to an aged and damaged artery. The wall is clogged with years of deposits; it is not as flexible as it was, it is no longer an efficient working part. An old stem cannot supply enough fluids from the roots to the top of the plant. This will limit the number of flowers and pleasure the plant gives us, as well as the ease with which it can reproduce. As the plant wants to reproduce, it supports any means to prevent this ageing process – how very human. In the wild that method is pruning by uncontrolled external influences. By removing much of the old stems the plant reduces the distance over which it has to carry fluids through old and internally damaged stems. It allows it to generate more young and virile stems from ground level.

To understand pruning it helps if we know how a plant grows. All the way along a stem there are little "nodes" that the leaves grow from. At each of these nodes there is an auxiliary bud. This type of bud grows into a new shoot. If a shoot has 20 sets of leaves along its length, then it has 20 auxiliary buds as well. Left unpruned, the plant will grow from the uppermost of these buds: in our example it will shoot from the twentieth bud first, that is, the highest one. This bud is on the thinnest uppermost part of the stem. The plant has to transport food for the bud to the very end of the stem. The shoot that grows from this point will be tall, subject to wind damage, and weak – it cannot be any fatter or stronger than the tip of the stem it is growing from.

If we know where the plant will grow from, we can understand that if we cut a length of the stem away, and leave four or five of these auxiliary buds on the stem, we solve all the potential problems of leaving a rose unpruned.

Now we can start pruning and get expert results. Please bear in mind that these comments on pruning are generalizations, and there will be circumstances where deviation is required to gain a specific result. First we need to set out our objectives to enable us to visualize the result:

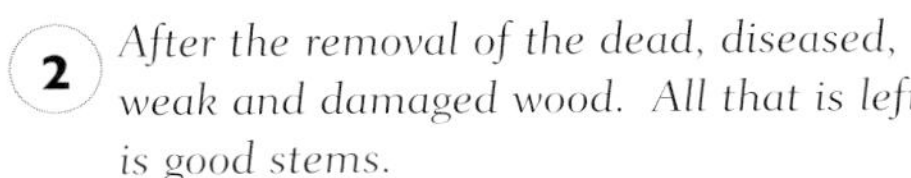

2 *After the removal of the dead, diseased, weak and damaged wood. All that is left is good stems.*

3 *The finished result after the good stems are pruned back.*

- To have a plant that is strong and healthy. Pruning will promote stronger, more vigorous growth, better able to resist disease.
- To create growth that will support plenty of flowers. Young, youthful and vigorous growth means an increased ability to flower.
- To stop the plant from getting leggy. When a plant is said to get leggy it means that there is a lot of old woody growth at the base of the plant, lacking leaf cover. It looks as if the productive bit of the plant is stuck up on stilts or legs. Pruning prevents this from happening and stops the plant getting taller and taller every year.
- To increase the productive lifespan of the plant. By promoting more young growth from low down, the amount of heavily aged wood is reduced, increasing the lifespan of the plant.

When to prune

This depends on climate. In warm areas pruning starts early, in cold climates it is later. Don't be tempted to start too early. After pruning, plants make new young shoots that are the future of the plant. You do not want to risk losing them to a late frost. The penalty for late pruning is minimal. In all areas the pruning window is approximately six weeks. The difference between pruning at the start and pruning at the end will be indiscernible in plant quality. All that happens is the early pruning will get the roses to bloom about four or five days earlier. Early pruning carries more risk of damage to the new shoots from a late frost. Be patient (which is one of nature's virtues) and wait until it is safe to prune. If your garden is in a frost pocket, wait and prune later. If your roses suffer from downy mildew in early spring, then try pruning a bit later – it will mean that there is less foliage at the time of an early attack, and as a result the plant may be more resistant. Finally, experiment: stagger your pruning and see what suits your garden best.

Best practice

Next we need a few notes on the general practical principles of pruning, applicable in nearly all circumstances.

1 *This shows some damaged wood that needs to be cut out.*

2 *Cut below the damage no matter how low you have to go.*

3 *The aim is to have a well-balanced rose with an open center and good shape.*

4 *When you cut through the stem the inside should be white. If there is brown discoloration cut the stem back further.*

- Always use good sharp secateurs. A sharp blade gives a clean cut and takes less effort.
- Try to make the cut about 1/2 in (1.25 cm) above an auxiliary bud.
- Make a sloping cut so that water will not sit on top of it or drain onto the auxiliary bud.
- Always cut out stems that are damaged.
- Try to prune into last summer's growth.
- Cut out any weak stems, making allowances for the fact that some varieties have more slender stems than others. Some have a heavy build, some a light framework.

Pruning specific types of plants

Let's start with newly planted roses. If you have planted bare-root roses in the spring, prune as follows.

- Bush roses (hybrid tea and floribunda). Cut all the stems down to about the length of your index finger.
- Patio and border roses. Prune to leave all the stems no longer than your forefinger.
- Climbing and shrub roses. Prune the stems down so that they are between 6 and 9 in (15 and 23 cm) tall.

Pruning established plants

All the general observations we have made up to now still apply with the additional requirement of visualizing how we want the plant to look. In our Utopian vision the plant is freely branching, well clothed with foliage, a neat and even shape, branches growing densely but without intermingling and damaging each other. All that remains is to turn our vision into a reality.

BUSH ROSES (HYBRID TEA AND FLORIBUNDA ROSES)

Gone are the old days when they needed to be reated in different ways. Modern floribunda roses can be treated identically to hybrid teas. It will make virtually no difference whether it is a plant that will grow up to 3 ft (1 m) or 6 ft (1.8 m) tall.

Examine the plant and picture in your mind's eye the way you want it to look in the summer. How does it look now? Is it lopsided, is it getting leggy or is it bushy? Is the center overcrowded? Does any dead, diseased or damaged wood need to be cut out?

1 *Pruning old established roses – before.*

2 *After the removal of the dead, damaged, diseased and weak growth.*

3 *The final result.*

Having imagined the shape we want to achieve, now is the time to start cutting. First take out dead wood because it is obviously useless – and the thorns on dead wood often hurt more than live thorns.

Next remove any weak growth.

Now remove anything that is clearly damaged. This includes cutting out any wood where the pith in the center of the stem is brown. Brown pith means a damaged stem. Keep cutting down until you get to white pith, even if you have to go all the way to the base of the plant.

Remove any growth that is old and looks past its "sell by date."

All that is left now is growth that has good potential. Check your mental picture of the shape of the plant and revise if necessary at this stage.

We now change tack, and select the best growths. They are the lovely strong branches that are young and full of vitality. Now comes the first tricky bit: identifying last year's growth. It is easy with practice. These stems had flowers last summer; they should start fairly low on the bush and will usually still be young looking, not brown and gnarled. When you find them, cut back hard, leaving them between 4 and 8 in (10 to 20 cm)long. Try to cut at an angle above an auxiliary bud. These buds are frequently spaced up the stem and are arranged in an alternate pattern. If you can see two buds, there will also be one on the other side of the branch, in between the two you can see.

Bear in mind that the top bud you leave is likely to grow a new shoot – the plant invariably shoots from the highest auxiliary bud on the stem. Make sure you cut to one that is pointing in roughly the direction you want it to grow in.

In the event that you are trying to rescue old roses you must behave differently. If roses have not had any pruning, or where the pruning was too light for many years, plants will have old wood, bare lower stems and unattractive, weak spindly top growth. You may have to cut into the old hard gnarled wood and hope that it will shoot.

Left: A shrub rose will have many cluster flowers at the same time. The effect is stunning when there are so many flowers together.

Above: Roses are great to mix with other plants – in this garden we can see climbing, shrub and hybrid tea roses.

(It doesn't always.) If you do try this, prune into the old wood at least two months earlier than you would normally, regardless of any frosts.

PATIO AND BORDER BUSH ROSES

These are more compact in their growing habit than other bush roses. The general mistake made in pruning is to think that because they are small plants they are delicate little specimens. A tendency to be gentle seems to spring to mind. Dispel that thought they are hardy and tough and love to be chopped down hard each year.

As the growing habit is to produce myriad densely packed stems from the base and for those stems to branch very freely, giving the rounded floriferous habit that we like, we do have to change the rules a little. With the multi-branching varieties it is not worth looking to see which direction a bud is pointing. There are so many, so close together that the law of averages wins out. Cut back hard and it will be fine. We can be less strict about crossing branches. After all they are compact, short plants, so the wind will not blow them about and rub the stems together. Cut back all the weak and damaged and dead wood, and all the strong stems from last year's growth to 3 to 5 in (8 to 13 cm). Trim the remainder to be neat and tidy, but not too overcrowded. Job done.

SHRUB ROSES

The pruning of these allows plenty of scope for individual freedom and choice. Some of the modern shrub roses can be pruned in the same way as bush roses (hybrid tea and floribunda), except you should be less severe, say, cutting off between half and two thirds of last season's growth.

The alternative way to treat most of the older shrub roses is different. You need to start in the same way by removing dead, diseased and very weak growth. The next step is to trim lightly, more like a haircut than a massacre. Trim to make it the size and shape that you want the plant to be. This allows the plant to adopt a dense, informal and soft shape that is frequently suited to these older varieties. Every four or five years you should prune harder to encourage young growth to regenerate from the base of the plant.

CLIMBING AND RAMBLING ROSES

It is common practice to prune these in early fall. This allows you to train new growth and prune at the same time. Doing two jobs at once seems like a good idea.

The important task with a climber is to get the structure covered. It is best to train branches in any direction except vertical (unless you want them to go straight up). On a wall take good strong branches and create a fan. Going up a pillar or post, train the stem to go round and round the post, forming a spiral. There is a reason for this aversion to the vertical. Earlier we looked at the way it is always the last auxiliary bud on the stem that grows. If your climber has a stem that goes up 6 to 10 ft (1.8 to 3 m), only the last bud on that stem will grow a shoot. The way we get the plant to grow from lots of the buds along the stem is by training the stem towards the horizontal and away from the vertical. When this happens most of the auxiliary buds will shoot out short flowering stems. By fanning, spiralling, bending and weaving we get the effect that we want – a framework covered in short flowering growths.

Now trim back the short flowering laterals to within an inch (2.5 cm) of the main stem. Train any new climbing shoots into a suitable gap in the framework. If possible, use a new shoot to replace one of the old ones. If the stems are too long, shorten them to make them fit the space you have. Try not to prune climbers too hard – this can cause lots of growth and very few flowers.

Below: Mature shrub rose "Nevada." This specimen is at least 9 ft (2.7 m) tall and 12 ft (3.6 m) wide.

Above right: Climbers can be used on different structures.
Below right: Many ramblers have dense clusters of small flowers.

bush rose

floribunda

Amber Queen

Bush Rose (Floribunda)

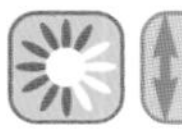
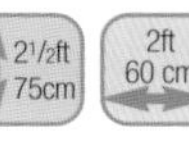

2ft
60 cm

FLOWER PROPERTIES ★★★★★

Color

I cannot think of another rose with such a pure color to its flower: clean, bright and a delightful deep amber. Only in the very hottest sun will we begin to see the depth of the color fade towards a golden yellow. Always excels in sunny sites; there can be some flower damage in wet climates.

Size and Shape

The buds are conical in shape, opening into cupped blooms with approximately 30 petals. The blooms average 2½ in (6.5 cm) in diameter.

Scent

Well perfumed; there are hints of apple and lemon in the fragrance.

Production

The flower clusters of have usually no more than five buds. The center bloom is always the largest but all are attractive. This is a variety that will begin to flower earlier than average in the season and repeats well throughout.

PLANT PROPERTIES ★★★★

Shape and Size

Short, compact and dense in its growing habit, it makes lots of basal growth and benefits from hard pruning. In very windy sites the weight of the flowers can be too much for the stems to hold upright. In most gardens expect a height of 2½ ft (75 cm) and 2 ft (60 cm) wide.

Position

Will thrive in any open position. Partial sunlight is acceptable.

Hardiness

Survives well in most regions. Avoid areas of low light levels.

FOLIAGE PROPERTIES ★★★★

Color

One of the additional beauties is the rich purple of the young foliage. It soon changes to green with bronze undertones.

Health Check

In very dry hot summers there may be some powdery mildew. Overall the health is good and if you keep the plant happy it will reward you.

Garden Uses

Anywhere, from mixed borders to formal rose gardens.

OVERALL ASSESSMENT ★★★★

✔ Color and ease of management in the garden.

✖ Needs correct location – avoid anywhere very windy. Flowers will be smaller if it is extremely sunny.

Baby Love

Bush Rose (Floribunda)

FLOWER PROPERTIES ★★★

Color

This is one of those flowers that leaves me speechless. The color is simple, bright yellow.

Shape and Size

The flowers are small, only 1 in (2.5 cm) across. They pop open very quickly from small round buds and very soon you have a fully open simple, single five-petalled flower.

Scent

There is no appreciable scent from the individual blooms.

Production

Generous in the production of flowers, maximizing the flowering season by starting to bloom early. The clusters have numerous buds. I find that there is little point in counting beyond 50 buds in a cluster, by then we know that there are a lot and that it will keep flowering well over a good period.

PLANT PROPERTIES

Shape and Size ★★★

Diminutive in stature. It develops into a small, rounded shrub and the shape is one of its assets, – with a rounded shape we get bloom low down. Unlikely to be above 2 ft (60 cm) tall in most areas and may well be as wide as it is tall.

Position

Will thrive in an open position where there is no exposure to cold winter winds.

Hardiness

Good in warm and hot regions. Not so hardy in cold areas.

FOLIAGE PROPERTIES ★★★★★

Color

The leaves are tiny and numerous, fully clothing the bush. The color is reassuring to look at, dark green and glossy – a combination that always makes for an attractive bush and contrasts well with the bright yellow flowers.

Health Check

Acclaimed as a healthy variety, specifically bred to be healthy. So far it is showing good resistance to disease.

Garden Uses

Try it in a pot, border or bed.

OVERALL ASSESSMENT ★★★★

✔ Health and neat, compact habit.
✖ Flowers over a good period.

Betty Boop
Bush Rose (Floribunda)

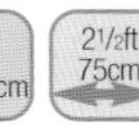

FLOWER PROPERTIES ★★★★★

Color
This is a bicolor: the flower is split into zones of contrasting color. The center is cream, while the edge of the flower has a carmine rim. As the flower ages the cream fades to be closer to white and the carmine intensifies, spreading towards the base of the petal. A tough flower, resistant to weather damage. In hotter sites the amount of red will increase more quickly as the flower ages.

Shape and Size
Plump buds open to reveal a tall, long flower with the carmine rim and cream below. The blooms open wide, more than 3 in (8 cm) in diameter, with 15 petals.

Scent
The perfume is light, somewhere between apple and aniseed.

Production
In this aspect there are no faults. The flowering season starts early and repeat bloom allows our enjoyment to continue to the very end of the season. The clusters have plenty of flowers; they are well spaced, opening over several days.

PLANT PROPERTIES ★★★★

Shape and Size
A compact and neat plant. It will provide a nice bushy specimen of even growth. In average conditions expect a height of 2½ ft (75 cm) and a width of 2 ft (60 cm).

Position
Very strong sunlight will affect the color. Otherwise anywhere in the garden.

Hardiness
Good in most regions. Give protection in severe winters.

FOLIAGE PROPERTIES ★★★

Color
Starting with a plum leaf that matures to dark green. A shine to the leaf leads us to expect good health.

Health Check
Overall a reliable performer but will require good culture to keep healthy. Blackspot can attack if the plant is under stress.

Garden Uses
Anywhere – in pots, tubs beds, borders. It is sure to be a pleasure.

OVERALL ASSESSMENT ★★★★

✔ The effect of the flowers and quantity of them.

✖ Weak perfume and imperfect health.

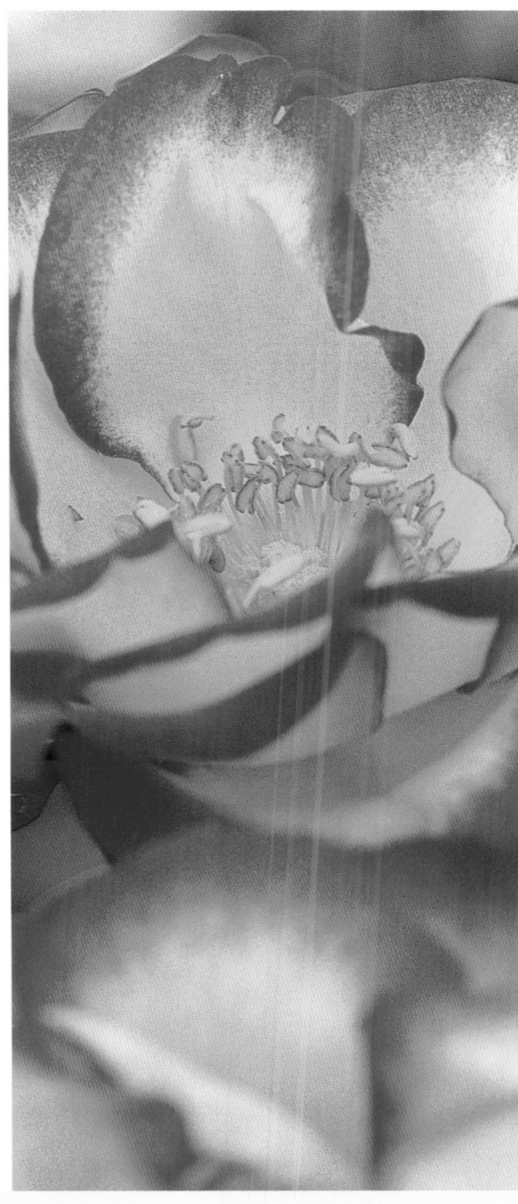

Betty Harkness

Bush Rose (Floribunda)

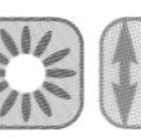

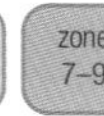

FLOWER PROPERTIES ★★★★★

Color

Tough to put into words but it is a tangerine with a little red added. It is powerful, attractive and striking. For such a strong shade it has a very stable color, hardly fading at all as the flower ages.

Shape and Size

The plump, dark green buds open to reveal a flower of exquisite beauty. Initially the flower has a classic shape with the ever desirable pointed bud, which opens slowly into a cupped flower. The size is good, at well over 3 in (8 cm) diameter, with more than 30 petals.

Scent

Strong and a delight. The classic sweet rose perfume.

Production

With clusters of up to nine buds, a prolific flower producer throughout the season – the recipe for a wonderfully colorful variety.

PLANT PROPERTIES ★★★★★

Shape and Size

This is a strong growing plant, without becoming difficult to manage. Producing plenty of basal shoots, it is easy to create a fine bush specimen. It will produce a bush that is about 3½ feet (1.1 m) tall and 2½ ft (75 cm) wide.

Position

No problem here, as long as it is a light position it will be happy.

Hardiness

A tough plant, it is worth trying in any region. Tolerates extremes remarkably well.

FOLIAGE PROPERTIES ★★★★

Color

Leaves are a very dark green, robust-looking and thick, giving a rich effulgent appearance.

Health Check

Not quite perfect but acceptable. Blackspot may appear when the plant is growing under stress.

Garden Uses

Anywhere a strong color is wanted. Traditional rose gardens or use as an individual accent.

OVERALL ASSESSMENT ★★★★

✔ Perfume and general good behaviour, also use as a cut flower.

✖ The color may be too strong for some schemes or tastes.

Cream Abundance

Bush Rose (Floribunda)

FLOWER PROPERTIES ★★★★★

Color

A combination of off-whites to creams intensifies towards the center of the flower. In very sunny conditions flowers fade before petal fall, but only to white, which is quite attractive. For a pale color the petals are very resistant to rain damage – brown spots are rare.

Shape and Size

Before opening the buds become plump and rounded. Initially a little flat, as the flower opens, the shape develops to a lovely circular one with more than 50 petals. It retains a tight center, thus extending the time of maximum beauty.

Scent

Pleasing perfume – a combination of myrrh and apple.

Production

A lot of flowers for the space consumed. Clusters of seven to nine buds open over a period of weeks and are rapidly followed by subsequent flushes of flower.

PLANT PROPERTIES ★★★★

Shape and Size

Growing to just below average height for a bush rose, it is bushy, compact and sturdy. Shoots from the base are strong and the flowering side shoots have plenty of rigidity to hold the flowers upwards. The plant produces a rounded form.

Position

It likes to thrive and will do so in most positions, even those that are challenging.

Hardiness

It will require some protection in the very coldest regions, but anywhere else is fine.

FOLIAGE PROPERTIES ★★★★★

Color

Exudes vitality and a desire to grow. The leaves are quite large and a rich dark green. They look wonderful on the plant, even when there are no flowers. They are a delectable contrast to the flowers.

Health Check

Resistance to ailments is good. As late season approaches some blackspot may be seen.

Garden Uses

Anywhere, from mixed borders to formal rose gardens.

OVERALL ASSESSMENT ★★★★

- ✔ All the components go together to make a wonderful plant.
- ✖ Not a popular color but one that brings out the best in mixed color schemes.

Easy Going

Bush Rose (Floribunda)

   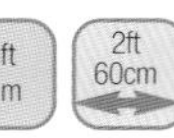

zone 7–8

FLOWER PROPERTIES ★★★★★

Color

Somewhere in the region that falls between amber and gold, this is a color that brings a smile to your face. It is rich and pure, restful yet bright. I am always astounded at the stability of the color in all weather conditions. As the flower ages there is a faint infusion of rose pink.

Shape and Size

The buds are light green, opening to reveal what appears to be a yet smaller bud, with the outer petals showing the slight pink hue that returns as the flowers die. From these unpromising buds the petals unfurl and enlarge to provide a divine flower in color and form. Upon maturity the flower will be up to 4 in (10 cm) in diameter, with 30 petals arranged in perfect symmetry.

Scent

The perfume is sweet and fruity, not the strongest but still a pleasure.

Production

A variety that enjoys flowering. It starts early in the season and finishes late. The clusters contain five or seven blooms, and they just keep on coming. Well worth using as cut flowers – after all, the bush will just produce more.

PLANT PROPERTIES ★★★★★

Shape and Size

A very neat and even bush. The flowers are held up on stems that have plenty of strength, growing to an even height and making a pretty rounded canopy. The plant will mature to be no more than 3 ft (1 m) tall and 2 ft (60 cm) wide.

Position

In all garden positions except shaded areas.

Hardiness

Thrives in all but the coldest regions, where it will survive, but will need winter protection.

FOLIAGE PROPERTIES ★★★★

Color

Light green foliage with a deep shine. The leaves are a nice size and provide an attractive foil to the flower color. Lots of leaves are produced, making it an attractive foliage plant.

Health Check

In most respects this is a very well-behaved variety. Where growing conditions make it vulnerable, downy mildew can affect it in the first half of the season.

Garden Uses

One to be put into mixed schemes, mixed borders or on its own.

OVERALL ASSESSMENT ★★★★

✔ One of the most beautiful to look at.

✖ Needs a location and growing method that will not encourage downy mildew.

Escapade

Bush Rose (Floribunda)

FLOWER PROPERTIES ★★★★

Color

A mixture of rose pink, blended with warm lilac and white. The warm lilac pink is arranged around the outer edge of the flower and the pure contrasting white at the center. In hotter conditions the pink becomes deeper as the flower ages.

Shape and Size

The buds are small, fresh and light green. They open slowly at first revealing the deeper color. Blooms become fully open imperceptibly, their 15 petals showing off their innocent beauty. At up to 3½ in (9 cm) across, these flowers delight the most demanding observer.

Scent

Fresh and sweet, with a traditional rose perfume.

Production

Flowers are produced with generosity. Clusters of up to 15 blooms keep the plant in full flower for weeks. This rose is very reliable at producing a good display late in the season. A lot of flower for the space used in the garden.

PLANT PROPERTIES ★★★

Shape and Size

A slightly more upright plant than average. The bush will be around 4 ft (1.2 m) tall, but no more than 2½ ft (75 cm) wide.

Position

An easy-to-grow garden plant, content in all but shady sites.

Hardiness

A variety that will not enjoy the coldest regions.

FOLIAGE PROPERTIES ★★★★

Color

Leaves are in the paler range of green with a matte sheen. They are fairly large but slightly more slender than average. Foliage cover is reasonable but not one of the most dense.

Health Check

A tendency to contract blackspot in the late season. But good tolerance to other malaises.

Garden Uses

Mixed with other species in a border or used on its own, it is a worthy addition to any planting scheme.

OVERALL ASSESSMENT ★★★★

✔ The enchanting beauty and innocence that it portrays.

✖ The plant is slightly upright and tends to become a little bare on the lower half, leaving too much stem on display.

Fellowship (Livin' Easy)

Bush Rose (Floribunda)

FLOWER PROPERTIES ★★★★★

Color

A strong deep burnished orange. When the sun shines on it there is an iridescent quality, surprising in such a deep color. One of the strengths of this variety is its ability to keep the color throughout the life of the flower. Come sun or rain, there is no noticeable fade or deterioration.

Shape and Size

Opening from mid green buds, the flower starts life as a pointed orange bud, from which petals unfurl. As it opens the flower transforms to a perfect circle with the petals in the center arcing inwards. With 30 petals and a flower averaging 3½ in (9 cm) across, we are delighted with a flower showing us beauty through all stages.

Scent

The distinct scent has traces of spice and myrrh.

Production

Clusters form in groups of five to seven blooms. They are very quick to repeat, giving an extended flowering period. Flowers are produced all over the top of the bush, providing maximum impact.

PLANT PROPERTIES ★★★★★

Shape and Size

This is a plant that always looks right. There are plenty of stems all growing to an even and regular pattern. Bushes are compact, strong and dense. As a mature plant it will be no more than 3½ ft (1.1 m) tall and 2½ feet (75 cm) wide.

Position

In all garden positions except shaded areas.

Hardiness

A tough variety, and one that is worth trying even in the most demanding locations.

FOLIAGE PROPERTIES ★★★★

Color

Mid to dark green with a deep shine. The leaves are large, exuding a willingness to perform. They are numerous on the plant, contributing to its appearance of vitality.

Health Check

A healthy variety that will give few problems. In adverse conditions it may suffer from a mild dose of either downy mildew or blackspot, but not enough to damage the plant.

Garden Uses

It will flourish in any garden situation.

OVERALL ASSESSMENT ★★★★

✔ The robust willingness to perform, masses of color.

✖ The color is strong and is not the easiest to combine in mixed plantings.

Greetings

Bush Rose (Floribunda)

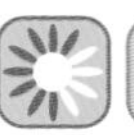

FLOWER PROPERTIES ★★★★

Color

Purple colors with random splashes of white near the center of the petals. A very stable color in all weather, which is rare for this shade.

Shape and Size

The flowers are only 2 in (5 cm) across and have 25 petals. They open quickly to be fairly flat and stay that way, smiling up at all who look at them.

Scent

There is a distinct scent with a hint of aniseed.

Production

Clusters can have up to 25 buds opening over a long period. The plant will be buried under its own display of flowers and there is an equally strong performance late in the season.

PLANT PROPERTIES ★★★★

Shape and Size

Below average height and bushy. No more than 3 ft (1 m) tall by 2 ft (60 cm) wide.

Position

Great in beds and borders.

Hardiness

A strong rose that will perform well in all conditions.

FOLIAGE PROPERTIES ★★★★

Color

Foliage is good with a deep lustre and a rich emerald color. Producing plenty to cover the plant, the leaves act as a pretty foil to the deep flower color.

Health Check

Adequate in most areas. Some powdery mildew in the second half of the season.

Garden Uses

Use in beds, borders and garden tubs.

OVERALL ASSESSMENT ★★★

✔ A great, deep color that keeps stable in sun.

✖ It lacks the strength of character that makes a fantastic rose.

Iceberg

Bush Rose (Floribunda)

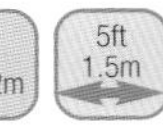

zone 6–7

FLOWER PROPERTIES ★★★★★

Color

It is nice to have a color that is easy to describe, one in which there is very little room for different interpretations. It is white. That sounds simple, until you realize how many different whites there are. This is the white of a fluffy cumulus cloud on a sunny day. It may take a light pink hue on some occasions.

Shape and Size

The buds are small and light green, opening to flowers of 2 1/2 in (6 cm) wide, or a little smaller in very hot conditions. Petals are shorter in the center of the bloom, giving a flat flower containing 25 petals.

Scent

The best description of the scent is "absent."

Production

Its strongest suit. Clusters of buds are massive and plentiful, opening over a few weeks. During that time there will be a sea of white flowers. With a quick cycle that allows it to repeat bloom, this rose gives a prodigious quantity of flower in the season.

PLANT PROPERTIES ★★★★

Shape and Size

The shape of the mature plant is lovely. It grows into a large rounded bush, always even and with good, low growth. At 4 to 7 ft (1.2 to 2.2 m) tall and 3 to 5 ft (1 to 1.5 m) wide this is a substantial garden rose.

Position

Grow in any position with good levels of light.

Hardiness

In spite of its slightly tender appearance, it is in fact hardy in all but the coldest regions.

FOLIAGE PROPERTIES ★★★

Color

Light green leaf with a promising shine to it. Leaves are a little on the small side and spread too thinly over the plant. The overall effect is that the plant looks sparse.

Health Check

Susceptible to powdery mildew. In poor conditions downy mildew may also be a problem.

Garden Uses

Grow as an individual specimen, as a hedge or in mixed borders.

OVERALL ASSESSMENT ★★★★

- ✔ The purity of the white blooms and the divine plant shape.
- ✖ The foliage lets it down, not entirely healthy and a little sparse.

L'Aimant (Victorian Spice)

Bush Rose (Floribunda)

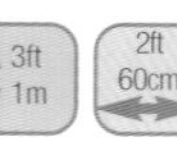

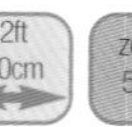

FLOWER PROPERTIES ★★★★★

Color

Rose pink with the subtlest tones of peach lightly added. The color fades as the flower ages and it may benefit from deadheading before the petals fall naturally.

Shape and Size

Well-rounded buds. The early flower shape has a long petal in bud form, opening to many shorter petals curling around the flower center. An attractive flower shape containing 50 petals in blooms often 3 in (8 cm) across.

Scent

This has to be one of the best. A complex blend of the finest rose scents, strong and addictively intoxicating.

Production

The clusters of flowers are usually no more than five buds. The center bloom is always the largest, but all are attractive. This variety begins to flower earlier in the season than average and repeats well throughout.

PLANT PROPERTIES ★★★★

Shape and Size

A strong and compact plant that consists of plenty of shoots from the base. When mature it will be 3 ft (1 m) tall and just over 2 ft (60 cm) wide.

Position

It is able to adapt to any open position. Partial sunlight is acceptable.

Hardiness

A strong variety suited to all regions.

FOLIAGE PROPERTIES ★★★

Color

There is plenty of foliage to make the plant look robust and lush. The leaves are fairly dark and shiny, providing an attractive effect.

Health Check

The main bugbear is a susceptibility to blackspot. Grow in good conditions to reduce the chance of an attack.

Garden Uses

A valuable addition to borders or beds. Remember to plant it where the perfume can be appreciated.

OVERALL ASSESSMENT ★★★★

- ✔ One of the best perfumes you can enjoy; also good as a cut flower.
- ✖ The flower can fade. Plant not 100 percent healthy.

Louisa Stone (Guinevere)

Bush Rose (Floribunda)

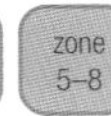

FLOWER PROPERTIES ★★★★

Color

An intricate blend of off-white to honey. The deeper shades are towards the center of the flower; there is a subtle gradation to the paler shades. The flower opens well in all but the wettest conditions.

Shape and Size

Round buds open to young flowers that start life as a pointed bud. This quickly changes to become a flower with complex and intricate arrangements of petals. With 40 petals, and a diameter of 3 in (8 cm) when fully open, the flower has beauty at every stage of its development.

Scent

Blessed with a pleasing perfume that has hints of apple and rose.

Production

Clusters average five blooms and there are usually plenty of them, making this a very productive and colorful garden plant. It has a short interlude between flushes of flower.

PLANT PROPERTIES ★★★★

Shape and Size

Below average size and with stems that can be a little on the lax side, the plant is thick and dense, with a shape that is closer to dome shaped than upright. A mature plant will grow no more than 3 ft (1 m) tall and around 2½ feet (75 cm) wide.

Position

Gives good results in all but the shadiest parts of the garden.

Hardiness

Will survive in cold regions if protected. Happy in hot regions.

FOLIAGE PROPERTIES ★★★★★

Color

Dark green with a slight bronze hue and very glossy. The leaves are large and there are lots of them. One of the leafier roses – the entire bush is well furnished with foliage from top to bottom.

Health Check

Resilient and reluctant to succumb to ailments. There may be minor infestations of blackspot at the end of the season.

Garden Uses

Mixed borders, beds or large patio planters.

OVERALL ASSESSMENT ★★★★

✔ Overall impression of vitality and well-being from leaf and flower.

✖ The lax stems can bend too much if the flowers are heavy or loaded with rain.

Margaret Merril

Bush Rose (Floribunda)

  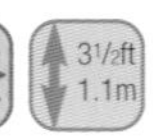 

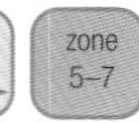

zone 5–7

FLOWER PROPERTIES ★★★★

Color

The overall impression is white, but it is not a pure white. The flower has a pearly pink center in the early stages of development. The intensity of the pink coloration varies from year to year depending on conditions that season. As the flower opens fully the pink disperses and the white dominates. Very good resistance to weather damage: heavy rain makes insignificant blemishes.

Shape and Size

A rare treat is in store with this rose. There are three distinct stages to the flower, and each is beautiful. It starts with an elegant pointed bud, ideal for cutting. At the second stage the pointed center remains but is surrounded by circles of perfect petals. Finally the center opens to reveal a pretty flower proudly showing off its stamens. All this is achieved from no more than 25 petals.

Scent

If I like the flower, it is nothing compared to the scent. Sweet rose and so strong, it must be in the top 10.

Production

Produced in small clusters, the plant has an adequate supply of flowers, but it is not a variety that covers every square inch with bloom. It repeats well in the late season.

PLANT PROPERTIES ★★★

Shape and Size

Bushes grow well, but do not willingly produce masses of new basal canes. This leads them to be more upright than average. The average height will be 3½ ft (1.1m) and a little more than 2 ft (60 cm) wide.

Position

Best to avoid heavy shade, which accentuates its tendency to grow up rather than out.

Hardiness

Quite hardy but not perfect. Protect well in cold regions.

FOLIAGE PROPERTIES ★★★★★

Color

The leaves are dark green with a good lustre to them. They are spaced out too much on the plant so it will never look fully clad. If allowed to grow too tall and leggy the bottom of the plant will be bereft of foliage.

Health Check

Blackspot is likely with this variety. Work on the assumption that prevention is better than cure.

Garden Uses

Provides the most wonderful cut flowers; works well in mixed beds or borders.

OVERALL ASSESSMENT ★★★★ 

✔ If you appreciate beauty in a flower and perfume, then it is a must-have.

✖ If you appreciate the easy life, then this rose is too much work to keep in good condition.

Mountbatten (Lord Mountbatten)
Bush Rose (Floribunda)

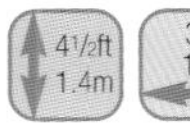

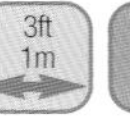

zone 6–7

FLOWER PROPERTIES ★★★★

Color

The main color is a deep mimosa yellow. This sometimes, but not always, adopts a pink flush as the flower ages. Firm petals give it excellent resistance to damage from wind and rain.

Shape and Size

The bud is well rounded and full of promise. Initially it is a high centered flower; as the bloom develops it opens to a wide flower, with shorter petals in the center. These will continue to arch towards the center. With over 45 petals and often 3 1/2 in (9 cm) across, it is a long-lasting pleasurable flower.

Scent

In the middle range as far as strength is concerned, featuring lemon, musk and honey aromas.

Production

The clusters are small, often no more than five buds to each. The flowers are held above the foliage on strong stems, and there are plenty of them, both for early and late season flowering.

PLANT PROPERTIES ★★★★

Shape and Size

A variety that obviously enjoys growing. The plant is strong, bushy and robust with plentiful strong basal shoots, making a vibrant bush up to 4 1/2 ft (1.4 m) tall and 3 ft (1 m) across.

Position

It is happy in most situations, including light shade. Avoid planting in dark areas.

Hardiness

Although it is tough, it will struggle unless given some protection in very cold areas.

FOLIAGE PROPERTIES ★★★★

Color

Prolific quantities of leaves are produced, which add to the vitality of the plant. They are nicely glossy, dark green and serrated edges.

Health Check

When the plant is kept in good condition it will reward you with exemplary behavior. Under stress blackspot may occur.

Garden Uses

Formal rose gardens, beds or mixed borders.

OVERALL ASSESSMENT ★★★★

✔ An able performer in all areas. The contrast between flower and leaf is attractive.

✖ While it is adequate in all respects it excels in none – a few more flowers would swing the balance.

Oranges 'n' Lemons

Bush Rose (Floribunda)

FLOWER PROPERTIES ★★★★

Color

There are two colors in this striped beauty, as the name implies. Orange is the basic flower color, with yellow added generously in bold stripes. It makes a flamboyant display in a vase or massed on the plant.

Shape and Size

Unlike many other novelty varieties there is no loss of flower size or form. Opening to 3½ in (9 cm) across and constructed of approximately 30 petals, the flower has plenty of substance to enhance its flamboyance.

Scent

The scent is a secondary feature compared to the visual interest.

Production

This variety has the ability to generate copious quantities of flowers. They come in clusters, neatly arranged above the foliage in the ideal position to exhibit their exotic colors. Quick to repeat bloom late into the season.

PLANT PROPERTIES ★★★★

Shape and Size

A willing performer that matures into a bushy plant. A satisfactory supply of basal shoots produces a plant of 4½ ft (1.4 m) tall and 3½ ft (1.1 m) wide.

Position

Good in sunny positions or light shade. Avoid medium to heavy shade.

Hardiness

Reasonable, but not perfect. Difficult in cold regions.

FOLIAGE PROPERTIES ★★★★

Color

There is a lot of leaf on the plant. Leaves are large, lush and closely spaced. Starting a pleasing shade of red and developing to dark green, they exude a sense of vitality.

Health Check

Provide good growing conditions and there will be little trouble. It can suffer either downy mildew or blackspot in adverse conditions.

Garden Uses

Somewhere in the spotlight to show off its extravagant color scheme.

OVERALL ASSESSMENT ★★★★

✔ A fine constitution for such a showy color.

✖ Better as an individual rather than in mixed planting schemes.

Pink Abundance

Bush Rose (Floribunda)

zone
5–7

FLOWER PROPERTIES ★★★★

Color

Deep rose-pink flowers. The color is warm, glowing in the sunshine and brightening a dull day. It is well behaved in nearly all weather conditions, although very strong sunshine can cause it to fade to a less attractive bluish pink. If this happens, just deadhead and enjoy the remaining flowers.

Shape and Size

Round buds open to provide flowers that retain a cupped shape, with petals that reflex to the center. They will never be large blooms, no more than 2 in (5 cm) across, containing 35 petals.

Scent

A light musk and lemon perfume.

Production

Many trusses of flowers are produced, with the buds close together in the truss. As the flowers open they will touch, giving complete coverage. Flowers continue to open in the truss for many days. With its admirably ability to repeat quickly, this variety has a long flowering season.

PLANT PROPERTIES ★★★

Shape and Size

Shorter than average, but produces an almost continuous supply of flowering stems. Compact and bushy, growing no more than 3 ft (1 m) tall by 2½ ft (75 cm) wide.

Position

Best in a reasonably open position, not too shady.

Hardiness

A strong plant, but it will not enjoy the coldest areas.

FOLIAGE PROPERTIES ★★★

Color

Copious foliage: dark shiny leaves crammed on the stems, so the plant will look solid and full of leaf.

Health Check

Reliable but not perfect. Under stress susceptible to either downy mildew or blackspot.

Garden Uses

In beds and rose gardens, or anywhere you need a splash of color.

OVERALL ASSESSMENT ★★★★

✔ The quantity of flower makes this one of the best.

✖ Watch it carefully to spot trouble and act immediately to keep it healthy.

Princess of Wales

Bush Rose (Floribunda)

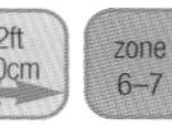

FLOWER PROPERTIES ★★★★★

Color

A bright, clean white that will almost dazzle in strong sunlight. On rare occasions it may have a slightly pink flush. For a white flower it resists rain damage well.

Shape and Size

The buds are round, opening to show a white conical flower, the outer petals wrapping around the others as if protecting them. Inner petals are shorter than the outer, so as the flower opens the final result is a flat bloom with several rows of petals neatly arranged on top of each other. Each flower is 2½ in (6 cm) wide with 35 petals.

Scent

There is gentle suggestion of rose and myrrh.

Production

Top marks are awarded here. The clusters are long lasting, with an average of nine buds that open in an orderly sequence. No sooner is one cluster over than the next is racing to take its place. Be disappointed if you don't get three flushes of flower in a season.

PLANT PROPERTIES ★★★

Shape and Size

A desirable growing habit. The bush generates plenty of growth, but it is controlled, forming a plant that is even in appearance and rounded in shape. The benefit of a rounded shape is that it allows flowers to be produced close to ground level. This rose flowers from just above ground to the top; it is only about 2½ ft (75 cm) tall and 2 ft (60cm) wide.

Position

Best results in positions with reasonable light, but it tolerates shade as well.

Hardiness

Give protection in the harshest regions and it will survive.

FOLIAGE PROPERTIES ★★★★★

Color

The leaves are mid green, large and numerous. The plant will be fully covered, with no gaps. The leaves have an understated look of durability to them, not glossy but with a rich patina.

Health Check

Excellent at repelling ailments. The only problem is the occasional outbreak of downy mildew.

Garden Uses

In patio planters, beds and borders. White always improves a mixed color scheme.

OVERALL ASSESSMENT ★★★★

- ✔ Purity of the color and copious flower production.
- ✖ Individual flowers could last a bit longer.

Purple Tiger

Bush Rose (Floribunda)

FLOWER PROPERTIES ★★★

Color

If you like something a little different this rose may suit you. The flower is decorated in radial stripes of purple and white. It may sound vulgar but it is both unusual and engaging.

Shape and Size

These flowers will never be big – expect no more than 2½ in (6 cm) across. With 25 petals the flower opens flat, which is the best shape to show off its stripes.

Scent

Enjoy a hint of spice and rose; pleasing without being strong.

Production

Flowers in clusters that are held prettily above the foliage; each cluster has up to 12 buds. Flowering is quick to repeat, so you don't have to wait long to decide whether you still like this eccentric flower.

PLANT PROPERTIES ★★★

Shape and Size

A short plant that will not often grow above 2½ ft (75 cm) tall. It is reasonably bushy.

Position

Plant somewhere where it will get a good amount of sun.

Hardiness

Best to avoid the coldest regions.

FOLIAGE PROPERTIES ★★★

Color

Leaves are a light green and a little more sparse on the plant than is desirable.

Health Check

In terms of roses with novelty flowers the health is good. Keep the growing conditions good to retain health.

Garden Uses

Mixed borders or somewhere where you want the eccentric.

OVERALL ASSESSMENT ★★★★

✔ The unusual flower.

✖ The foliage and plant are not up to a very high standard.

Remembrance

Bush Rose (Floribunda)

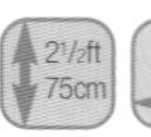

FLOWER PROPERTIES ★★★★★

Color

An iridescent bright scarlet almost as bright as a field of poppies. The flowers are impervious to the effects of either a burning sun or a heavy storm.

Shape and Size

The flowers pop out of rounded buds, mimicking the shape of the bud in the early stages. Rounded blooms show the reverse of the outer petals. The inner rows of petals mass prettily together in circular rows. With 45 petals and at no more than 2½ in (6 cm) across, there are many petals packed into the flower.

Scent

This rose is all show – a show to see, not to smell.

Production

It would be unreasonable to fault it. Produces abundant, well-spaced clusters to cover the surface of the plant, and open over a long time, extending the flowering period to the maximum. Then it has the audacity to repeat bloom and do it all again.

PLANT PROPERTIES ★★★★

Shape and Size

Makes a framework of shoots that allow a rounded shape to develop as the plant matures. It will never become very tall, probably no more than 2½ ft (75 cm), with a girth of 2 ft (60 cm).

Position

A truly utilitarian rose for every position.

Hardiness

With protection in the coldest areas it should survive. It will be happy elsewhere.

FOLIAGE PROPERTIES ★★★★

Color

Small leaves, with lots of serrations around the edges. Emerald green in color with a polish that would be the envy of any cabinetmaker. The leaves are close to each other on the stem, festooning the whole plant.

Health Check

When under stress downy mildew may attack. Other problems will be negligible.

Garden Uses

Beds, borders and low hedges. Anywhere for a stunning impact.

OVERALL ASSESSMENT ★★★★

✔ A colorful flower on a manageable, well-behaved plant.

✖ Grow in good conditions or downy mildew will be a problem.

Scentimental

Bush Rose (Floribunda)

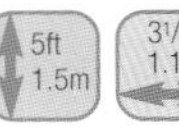

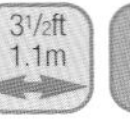

zone
6–8

FLOWER PROPERTIES ★★★★★

Color

Two distinct colors make a dramatic statement. Claret red predominates, with stripes and splashes of white all over. Unlike many bicolor roses, this one retains a clear definition of its two colors until the petals fall. The intricate color patterns are undamaged by rain or strong sunshine.

Shape and Size

The buds are medium size and start with a delectable pointed center. As they develop further the large petals open to show off a bloom fully 3 in (8 cm across, with a count of up to 30 petals.

Scent

The perfume is a strong, sweet, spicy combination that infuses the area around the plant.

Production

Many novelty varieties are reluctant to bloom freely. This is an exception, providing fine clusters in generous quantities, enough to cover the plant in blooms in the early season. With strong late season blooming as well, there are months of pleasure to enjoy.

PLANT PROPERTIES ★★★

Shape and Size

Its habit of branching out from the base in a profligate manner guarantees a bushy plant. Strong stems ensure that the flowers are held upright as the plant grows to between 3 and 5 ft (1 and 1.5 m) tall. Expect it to be in the region of 2 to 3½ ft (75 cm to 1.1 m) wide

Position

A quality performer in all but the shadiest spots of the garden.

Hardiness

Protection is required in the coldest regions, otherwise it will be happy.

FOLIAGE PROPERTIES ★★★★★

Color

Luxuriant, dark green leaves give the plant an aura of success. Not only are the leaves large, they are closely packed along the stem making the plant an attractive spectacle before it blooms.

Health Check

As long as the plant is not growing under stress it will be trouble free. In adverse conditions it can be mildly susceptible to blackspot

Garden Uses

Plant it where it can show off its extrovert flowers.

OVERALL ASSESSMENT ★★★★

✔ A novelty flower on a very fine plant.

✖ It may get just a bit bigger than we would like.

Sexy Rexy

Bush Rose (Floribunda)

FLOWER PROPERTIES ★★★★★

Color

A bright and iridescent rose pink. The buds are a slightly deeper shade when first open. Retains its color well and is able withstand a beating from wind and rain without appreciable damage.

Shape and Size

Not the largest of flowers, only up to 3 in (8 cm) across, in spite of having at least 40 petals each. Buds will be rounded and plump. With short petals in the center of the flower it develops into an open bloom with a low flower center crowded with petals .

Scent

A variety that provides a visual display not an aromatic experience.

Production

There are few rivals in the competition to provide ample flowers. Clusters abound, with each containing up to 45 buds. As the flowers open in sequence the display is both dense and long lasting. This performance will be repeated late in the season.

PLANT PROPERTIES ★★★

Shape and Size

Short, compact and dense in its growing habit. Makes lots of basal growth and benefits from hard pruning. In very windy sites the weight of the flowers can be too much for the stems to hold upright. In most gardens expect a height of 2½ ft (75 cm) tall and 2 ft (60 cm) wide.

Position

Will thrive in any open position if not too windy. Partial sunlight is acceptable

Hardiness

Survives well in most regions.

FOLIAGE PROPERTIES ★★★★★

Color

One of the additional beauties is the rich purple of the young foliage. It soon changes to green with bronze undertones.

Health Check

In very dry, hot summers there may be some powdery mildew. Overall the health is good; keep the plant happy and it will reward you by staying healthy.

Garden Uses

Anywhere, from mixed borders to formal rose gardens.

OVERALL ASSESSMENT ★★★★

✔ Good color and ease of management in the garden.

✖ Needs correct location – avoid anywhere very windy or sunny.

Simply the Best

Bush Rose (Floribunda)

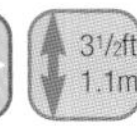

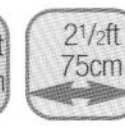

FLOWER PROPERTIES ★★★★

Color

Amber, peach and pink combinations. The deeper and pink shades increase as the flower ages in hot sunshine. Withstands rain damage.

Shape and Size

Smallish flowers. With more than 50 petals arranged in neat patterns and swirls, the 2 in (6 cm) blooms are packed with interest.

Scent

Light and pleasing, with a hint of citronella.

Production

Long-lasting, numerous flowers. With a dense display in both early and late season, a veritable feast of color is promised.

PLANT PROPERTIES

Shape and Size ★★★★

This plant is eager to grow, producing basal shoots that are strong and frequent. It is bushy and retains an even shape. Growing to 3½ ft (1.1 m) tall and 2½ ft (75 cm) wide, it makes a perfect garden plant.

Position

Will thrive in any open position. Partial sunlight is acceptable.

Hardiness

It might not thrive in the coldest regions.

FOLIAGE PROPERTIES

Color ★★★★

The foliage is dark and exudes vigor. There is plenty of it on all the stems – the plant is well furnished from top to toe.

Health Check

When grown in good conditions there will be very few problems.

Garden Uses

An asset in any garden situation.

OVERALL ASSESSMENT

★★★★

✔ An excellent performer combining a good flowering ability with abundant luxuriant foliage.

✖ A slightly more definite color would be an improvement.

bush rose
hybrid tea

Big Purple

Bush Rose (Hybrid Tea)

zone 5–8

FLOWER PROPERTIES ★★★★

Color

The name is a bit of a giveaway. This is a deep red that has purple as a dominant feature. In the young flower it is very attractive, but as the flower ages the color loses its beauty. Deadhead to keep the plant looking tidy.

Shape and Size

Another giveaway: it is Big. With 45 petals and developing to 5 in (13 cm) across, this is a monster of a flower. The shape is all that you could desire from a large-flowered hybrid tea.

Scent

A strong, sweet rose experience that you are sure to enjoy.

Production

One of the weaker points – there will never be really dense flower cover. Adequate in the first flush and light in the late blooming.

PLANT PROPERTIES ★★★

Shape and Size

The plant is tall, growing to 4½ ft (1.4 m) and 2½ ft (75 cm) wide. It will tend to become a little leggy with bare stems on the lower parts of the plant.

Position

Give it sun, but not too much intense midday sun.

Hardiness

Not suitable for very cold areas or windy sites.

FOLIAGE PROPERTIES ★★★★★

Color

The leaves are big, but the color is a slightly dull grey green. They may be absent on the lower reaches of a mature plant.

Health Check

Keep your eye open for ailments and act quickly to stop them spreading. Mildew and Blackspot will attack a stressed plant.

Garden Uses

Rose beds and borders.

OVERALL ASSESSMENT ★★★★

- ✔ The outstanding color and good perfume.
- ✖ Not healthy enough to be a trouble-free pleasure.

Elina (Peaudouce)

Bush Rose (Hybrid Tea)

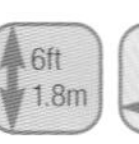

FLOWER PROPERTIES ★★★★

Color

This is a pale rose, ranging from almost white to lemon sorbet. The deeper coloring is in the center of the flower. Unlike many pale-colored varieties this is a good performer in all weather: hot, cold or wet, the flower is clean and fresh.

Shape and Size

It is obvious from the appearance of the buds, which are large and pointed, that we are about to enjoy a large flower. Initially the petals intertwine into a classic, long pointed bud. As it opens the flower becomes more rounded, but spectacular – often more than 5 in (13 cm) across with 45 petals.

Scent

There are so many good aspects to this rose, but it is lacking in perfume.

Production

Considering the sheer size of the flowers, it is able to produce a prodigious quantity in a season. Repeat flowering keeps the flowers going until late. Their long, straight stems make them good for cutting.

PLANT PROPERTIES ★★★

Shape and Size

The bush matches the flower: it is big, strong and bold with plenty of strong growth from the base. Expect it to be between 4 and 6 ft (1.2 and 1.8 m) tall extending between $2\frac{1}{2}$ and $3\frac{1}{2}$ ft (75 cm and 1.1 m) wide.

Position

Good for borders or beds where height is required.

Hardiness

Just as you would expect from such a strong grower, it thrives in all areas.

FOLIAGE PROPERTIES ★★★★★

Color

In a similar way to the plant and flower, it produces big, strong leaves. They are dark green and there are lots of them, covering the substantial plant. Absolutely in keeping with the other features of the rose.

Health Check

A fine reputation for having a robust constitution that will repel any attacks to its health. In good conditions it will remain completely healthy.

Garden Uses

Makes a hedge, bed or a feature.

OVERALL ASSESSMENT ★★★★

- ✔ Tough and easy, with robust health. It will keep its leaves through a mild winter.
- ✖ Flowers tend to sit near the top on long stems, leaving lots of plant below.

Ingrid Bergman

Bush Rose (Hybrid Tea)

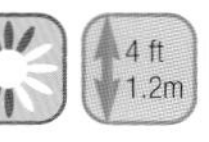

zone 5–7

FLOWER PROPERTIES ★★★★★

Color

Here we have the color that epitomizes love: a deep red with an almost velvet quality. How we love to give or receive a dozen of these red roses. The color is stable, fading only in hot climates. It can suffer some spotting in wet conditions

Shape and Size

Large and bold without being vulgar. The bud is pointed and retains its classical shape for several days. With 45 large petals, it takes a few days to develop into a fully open bloom, which can be more than 4 in (10 cm) across.

Scent

There is a haunting sweetness to the perfume.

Production

The flowers usually come as large individuals. Where they appear in clusters, the first flower is the major event, the others will be smaller in the role of a supporting act, but still lovely. With a good ability to repeat bloom, this rose gives pleasure for a long time every year, in the garden or as a cut flower.

PLANT PROPERTIES ★★★★

Shape and Size

A strong growing plant that produces plenty of thick canes from the base. It acquires a bushy habit as it matures to about 4 ft (1.2 m) tall and 2½ ft (75 cm) wide.

Position

Avoid extremes, very intense sunny positions or heavy shade.

Hardiness

It may look tough but it will not enjoy life in very cold areas.

FOLIAGE PROPERTIES ★★★

Color

Starting out red and turning to dark green, the leaves are robust and plentiful, having all the visual qualities to match the strengths of the plant.

Health Check

No troubles early in the season. Later it can suffer from blackspot.

Garden Uses

A fine rose to use in beds, on its own or in mixed plantings.

OVERALL ASSESSMENT ★★★★

✔ An arresting and seductive color allied to a distinguished perfume.

✖ Can be a bit fussy and performs much better in its ideal conditions.

Just Joey

Bush Rose (Hybrid Tea)

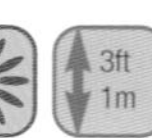

FLOWER PROPERTIES ★★★★

Color

In ideal conditions there are few better colors. Blend copper and peach together to picture this rose's warm tone. Unfortunately, in hot regions the color will be less awe-inspiring, becoming pale and washed out.

Shape and Size

Tall buds open with long petals. The flower evolves into wide, cupped blooms; the large petals are curved and elegant with scalloped edges. There never seems to be enough petals – about 30 in all – but it doesn't matter. The flower is large, 4 1/2 in (11 cm) across, and beautiful.

Scent

Strong, with the sweetness of a favorite rose perfume.

Production

A variety that provides some of the earliest flowers of the season. Borne in small clusters, with the first bloom having greater stature than the others, the early flowering is spectacular. Strong fall flowering follows.

PLANT PROPERTIES

Shape and Size ★★★

Do not expect anything too big. This plant will be short, no more than 3 ft (1 m) tall. It grows branches that spread out wide, so in spite of the low height it will still be up to 2 1/2 ft (75 cm) wide. There are not quite enough stems to make a dense bush and it can often look a little sparse.

Position

Grow in good conditions. Do not plant in heavy to medium shade.

Hardiness

This is not the hardiest rose and will not thrive in very cold regions.

FOLIAGE PROPERTIES ★★★

Color

The leaves have a pleasing appearance. Their color is deep and reassuring, and the upper surface greets you with a deep shine. Although they are large, they are spaced out on the stem so the plant looks a little bare.

Health Check

Imperfections are not always disastrous and the likelihood is that powdery mildew and blackspot will attack in the late season. Both are controllable with good culture and careful management of the plant.

Garden Uses

In rose beds and mixed borders.

OVERALL ASSESSMENT ★★★★

✔ The flower is too lovely to be ignored.

✖ The plant is not as lovely as the flower and requires work to get the best from it.

Marilyn Monroe

Bush Rose (Hybrid Tea)

FLOWER PROPERTIES ★★★★★

Color

A blend of apricot and cream that is so gorgeous it looks edible. The pale shades around the outside of the bloom blend irresistibly with the richer apricots of the flower center. The intensity of color at the flower center draws our attention away from the soft outer areas of the flower. In spite of this soft and gentle appearance the flowers are robust with firm petals that resist damage from rain with ease. In very sunny conditions the outer petals will begin to fade, but will not burn or scorch.

Shape and Size

The petals swirl and curl into the prettiest hybrid tea shape. With 30 petals to each flower there is plenty of substance to keep the shape for several days. Expect it to open to 3½ in (9 cm) across when mature.

Scent

There is a light and mild, fresh perfume that is neither absent nor overwhelming.

Production

Small clusters of no more than five buds; an abundance of shapely flowers both in early and late season. The flowers are always produced on long stems that keep the blooms looking upwards.

★★★

PLANT PROPERTIES

Shape and Size

A very well-behaved plant that grows to around 3½ ft (1.1 m) tall and 2½ ft (75 cm) wide. The shape is neat and even, and flowers are held proudly over the roundded bush.

Position

A good performer in all areas; it is especially fond of hot weather and will flourish in full sunlight.

Hardiness

Survives well in most regions. Avoid areas of low light. ★★★★★

FOLIAGE PROPERTIES

Color

One of the additional beauties is the rich purple color of the young foliage. It soon changes to green, with bronze undertones.

Health Check

In very dry, hot summers there may be some powdery mildew, but that should be your only concern. Overall the health is good, and if you keep the plant happy it will reward you.

Garden Uses

Anywhere, from mixed borders to formal rose gardens. ★★★

OVERALL ASSESSMENT

✔ The color and shape of the flowers will bring immense satisfaction.

✖ It could produce a few more flowers.

New Zealand

Bush Rose (Hybrid Tea)

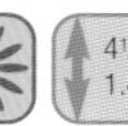

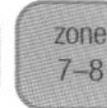

FLOWER PROPERTIES ★★★★

Color

This is a pale pink, deepening towards the outside of the flower. It is not the most inspiring color and may best be described as gentle and soft. Rain can cause some discoloration to the soft petals.

Shape and Size

Produces big flowers although each has only 35 petals. All the flowers will be the same: large, high-pointed centers in the classical form, reaching 4 in (10 cm) across.

Scent

The real reason to grow this rose is its perfume. It is almost too strong to be real, but too beautiful to be artificial.

Production

The large flowers will be single blooms or in small clusters. In clusters there will be only one large flower and three or four smaller blooms. Producing a respectable volume of flowers in both early and late season, it will satisfy without excelling.

PLANT PROPERTIES ★★★

Shape and Size

The plant is more upright than average maturing to 4½ ft (1.4 m) tall and 3½ ft (1.1 m) wide. It branches from the base, which helps to maintain a strong and virile plant.

Position

Needs reasonable light. Any areas of heavy shade should be avoided.

Hardiness

Will not survive in cold regions without thorough protection.

FOLIAGE PROPERTIES ★★★★★

Color

Leaves are big and bold, growing in good quantity from the top to low down on the plant. They inspire confidence with their rich green color and lacquered shine.

Health Check

Health is unexpectedly good; plants resist most attempted infestations. There can be some powdery mildew late in the season.

Garden Uses

In rose beds and borders, where the scent can be enjoyed.

OVERALL ASSESSMENT ★★★★

✔ Perfume and good overall behavior.

✖ The color could be more inspirational. A little light in flower production.

Paul Shirville (Heart Throb)

Bush Rose (Hybrid Tea)

FLOWER PROPERTIES ★★★★★

Color

At first glance the eye sees a pink rose, verging on salmon pink. Looking more deeply into the flower we pick up a complex blend of colors, ranging from a dash of yellow, through a spectrum of pinks to the salmon pinks. It is the way the colors mix together that produce the final result – one where the color positively radiates out.

Shape and Size

The formation of the flower is exquisite at all stages. Starting with a high-centered bud, the petals curl seductively around, forming an elegant point. The flower can open to be more than 3½ in (9 cm) wide and still maintain a pointed center with its petals reflexing enticingly.

Scent

As sweet and strong as the flower is beautiful. The perfume is a classic rose scent.

Production

Produced either as single blooms or in groups of up to five, flowers are plentiful on the plant and make a strong display. The plant produces repeat blooms throughout the season. Cut them for the house to encourage the plant to produce even more flowers.

PLANT PROPERTIES ★★★★

Shape and Size

The quality of the plant allows this variety to produce many flowers. It grows with enthusiasm and will be well branched, reaching up to 4½ ft (1.4 m) tall and 3½ ft (1.1 m) wide.

Position

Suited to any reasonable garden site. Avoid heavy shade.

Hardiness

Robust enough to withstand all but the most severe climates.

FOLIAGE PROPERTIES ★★★

Color

The attractive young foliage develops into large dark green leaves. They provide the plant with a moderately full covering. In an ideal world there would be a few more.

Health Check

Only moderate resistance to common problems. It will require protection from blackspot, and if conditions are adverse it may suffer from downy mildew.

Garden Uses

Ideal for rose gardens or in a display all of its own.

OVERALL ASSESSMENT ★★★★

✔ A flower that will provide joy and happiness every year.

✖ The foliage is the weak point and it is not impervious to disease.

Perception (Le Ann Rimes)

Bush Rose (Hybrid Tea)

zone 7–9

FLOWER PROPERTIES ★★★★★

Color

Two contrasting colors make an appealing flower. The bulk of the petal is a golden cream; around the upper edge it is rose pink, which looks as if it has been sprayed onto the petal. The combination is very effective and one of the wonders is how it can produce so many identical flowers when every one looks as if it was hand painted.

Shape and Size

Long conical buds. Petals unfurl slowly allowing us to enjoy the elegant pointed bud. As the flower approaches middle age the outer petals form a perfect circle, while the inner petals still hold their high-centered point. When it reaches its fullest extent you can expect a flower of at least 5 in (13 cm) in diameter. It retains form and shape, yet has only 35 petals. Excellent in wet conditions.

Scent

Enjoy exploring the powerful scent, which is sweet, with a combination of rose and lemon.

Production

As is typical of pure hybrid tea roses, the flowers will often be borne as single blooms. They are on long straight stems, just perfect for cutting. Produces plenty of flowers and repeats quickly and continuously into the late season.

PLANT PROPERTIES

Shape and Size ★★★

Lots of vigor, maybe too much. The plant will throw up strong canes and, depending on conditions, may grow to between $4\frac{1}{2}$ and 8 ft (1.4 to 2.5 m) tall. It will never become exceedingly bushy; expect $2\frac{1}{2}$ to $3\frac{1}{2}$ ft (75 cm to 1.1 m) wide. It can be kept under control by hard winter pruning – then after flowering, don't just deadhead, give it a moderate summer pruning.

Position

Grows with enthusiasm in any site. In a shady position it may get taller, growing up to look for light.

Hardiness

It is tough and if it gets damaged usually has the vigor to grow again.

FOLIAGE PROPERTIES ★★★

Color

The leaves are in proportion with the plant – that is, large. They are some of the most leathery-looking leaves you will see. Tough, thick and strong in a rich green color. Plenty are produced to give the plant a good covering.

Health Check

The main adversary of this variety is blackspot. Some measure of protection will be required.

Garden Uses

Only in positions that can cope with the size of the plant.

OVERALL ASSESSMENT ★★★★

- ✔ This is the easiest way to grow a vase full of perfect blooms, and they have a good perfume.
- ✖ You may need a ladder to pick the flowers in some areas. Not as healthy as many other roses.

Poetry in Motion (Gift of Life)

Bush Rose (Hybrid Tea)

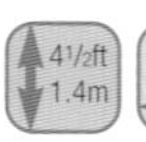

FLOWER PROPERTIES ★★★★★

Color

Saffron yellow suffused with pink as the flower ages. The color is cheerful and the injection of pink as the flower ages is not overpowering – only a light dusting to accompany the last few days of the flower.

Shape and Size

Large flowers spring out of long buds. This is a variety with poise and elegance. In the early stages the petals are draped around the tight high-centered flower in distinct-sculptured curves. As the flower develops, the length of the petals becomes evident. Retaining its attractive shape the flower will be more than 4 in (10 cm) across, containing up to 35 petals.

Scent

Pleasant perfume with hints of citrus and honey.

Production

The large flowers are held individually or in clusters of no more than five buds. Repeat blooms quickly, so there are plenty of flowers to enjoy. Wonderful for cutting or in the garden.

PLANT PROPERTIES ★★★★

Shape and Size

As with all good roses, it produces a nice, even plant. Growth is vigorous, but not excessive. It will be between 3 and 4½ feet (1.1 and 1.4m) tall, and around 3 ft (1 m) wide.

Position

Thrives in all but the shadiest positions.

Hardiness

Successful in all but the coldest regions.

FOLIAGE PROPERTIES ★★★

Color

Big leaves that look as if they have just returned from the beauty parlor, their gloss is so bright. They are mid green, having grown through a youthful period of plum red. More than enough to cover the plant, creating a striking sight before the flowers arrive.

Health Check

Nothing is perfect, and this is no exception. Powdery mildew is its Achilles' heel.

Garden Uses

A valuable addition in any rose garden, bed or mixed border.

OVERALL ASSESSMENT ★★★★

✔ A prolific producer of enchanting flowers.

✖ We may have to put up with a bit of powdery mildew.

Pride of England

Bush Rose (Hybrid Tea)

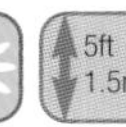

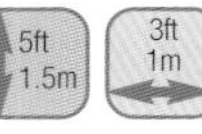

FLOWER PROPERTIES ★★★

Color

Deep blood red. The outer petals are almost black. The color lasts very well in all but the hottest sunshine. In very hot areas plant where there is some relief from intense sunlight.

Shape and Size

Classic in every detail – the petals intertwine in concentric circles creating the high center of the flower. As it opens the petals continue to unfurl, their size increasing, but retaining the flower shape. Eventually all 35 petals will be on display. The bloom reaches 4 in (10 cm) across, and we will have had days of pleasure watching its progress.

Scent

The perfume is light and distinctive, undertones of spice are present.

Production

Perfect buds are produced on perfect long stems. An abundance of blooms continues throughout the season. Unlikely to produce clusters with more than three buds, but there are still plenty of flowers to make a dramatic impact.

PLANT PROPERTIES ★★★

Shape and Size

A strong plant that produces a multitude of basal growth that ensures the plant will be wide and bushy. It will grow to an even height – expect 4 to 5 ft (1.2 to 1.5 m) tall and about 3 ft (1m) wide.

Position

Anywhere except very strong sunlight in hottest areas

Hardiness

Moderate; not one to try in the colder regions.

FOLIAGE PROPERTIES ★★★★★

Color

The leaf is unusual, mid green underscored with a faint purple hue, and with a matte finish. There will always be plenty of leaf to give good coverage over the plant.

Health Check

For a dark red rose its health is good. It only suffers from blackspot in adverse conditions.

Garden Uses

It will add stature to a rose garden or be a focal point in a mixed border.

OVERALL ASSESSMENT ★★★★

- ✔ A reliable deep red rose, good for cut flowers in the house.
- ✖ It would benefit from more perfume and a brighter color.

Remember Me

Bush Rose (Hybrid Tea)

FLOWER PROPERTIES ★★★★

Color

An intriguing shade that explores the realms of copper and bronze. It is wonderful and unique but discolors badly in extremely hot sun.

Shape and Size

The shape is straight from the classic high-centered school. It opens its 35 petals, faultlessly maintaining the structured form. When fully developed it is more than 3 1/2 in (9 cm) wide.

Scent

This rose is not grown for perfume; the color is novel enough to forgive the absence of fragrance.

Production

Buds are produced in a combination of single blooms and clusters of up to five. They are numerous on the plant and, while the bush is never completely covered, the unexpected and rare color will still amaze passers-by.

PLANT PROPERTIES ★★★★

Shape and Size

For one of the novelty colors the plant is excellent, growing with strong branches from the base to make a nice even bush of 3 1/2 ft (1.1 m) tall and 2 1/2 (75 cm) ft wide.

Position

Any position will grow a good plant. A little shade from the most intense sun is helpful.

Hardiness

Not ideal in the coldest regions.

FOLIAGE PROPERTIES ★★★★★

Color

Light green and very shiny. The production of leaves is prolific, making the plant look full of vigor even on the lower parts of the bush.

Health Check

A report might say "good effort, could try harder." There can be blackspot attacks if the plant is under stress.

Garden Uses

Rose beds, borders or somewhere for an unusual color.

OVERALL ASSESSMENT ★★★

✔ The color in the garden or as a cut flower.

✖ You will have to keep on top of disease control to get the very best results.

Renaissance (Cameo Perfume)

Bush Rose (Hybrid Tea)

FLOWER PROPERTIES ★★★★★

Color

Shades that graduate from white to blush pink. The outer petals possess the paler tones, the center of the flower the pearl and blush shades. Petals resist damage from all but the heaviest rain.

Shape and Size

As the buds begin to open they form the most perfect of flower shapes. Looking so delicate a flower could easily be mistaken for the finest porcelain with its high center and perfect circles of petals. When fully open the flower is large at 3 1/2 in (9 cm) across, but has only 25 petals to create this immaculate shape.

Scent

Powerful and pleasurable, with strong aromas of rose, citronella and honey.

Production

Flowers are either single or in clusters of no more than three buds. It is fortunate that each flower lasts well, otherwise the flowering density would be too low. Repeats well in the late season.

PLANT PROPERTIES ★★★

Shape and Size

Makes a bush that has branches spreading out wide. It will not get very tall, no more than 3 ft (1 m), often less, with a width of 2 ft (60 cm).

Position

It is happiest in sun, but will perform adequately in semi shade.

Hardiness

In contrast to the delicate appearance of the flower, the plant is hardy and worth a try in all regions.

FOLIAGE PROPERTIES ★★★★★

Color

The leaves are big, a little too large for the size of the plant. They form more easily on the upper half of the plant, on occasions leaving the bottom section a little bare. Dark green with a matte finish, they contrast with the flowers perfectly.

Health Check

Lacking in ideal behavior. Powdery mildew is likely in the second half of the season; blackspot will take advantage if the plant is stressed.

Garden Uses

Where the perfume will be appreciated.

OVERALL ASSESSMENT ★★★★

✔ A flower that epitomizes all the virtues of the rose.

✖ A plant that cannot resist all the vices of a rose.

Royal William (Fragrant Charm)

Bush Rose (Hybid Tea)

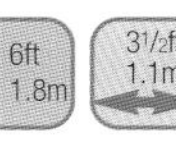

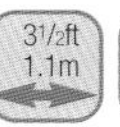

FLOWER PROPERTIES ★★★★

Color

While the flower is young it is a rich deep crimson. It behaves impeccably with no sign of scorching in the sun and very little damage from rain. As the bloom reaches its final few days the color fades, adopting a less attractive bluish red tinge. Best to deadhead at this stage.

Shape and Size

Flowers are large enough to satisfy all but the unreasonably demanding. With a shape that is a little on the rounded side, there are more than 45 petals in the flower. It opens to an impressive 4½ in (11 cm) across.

Scent

Rewarding without excelling. The flower color leads us to anticipate a stronger perfume.

Production

A rose with larger-than-average flowers often lets itself down by not producing enough. This plant is an exception. The flowers are sometimes single or sometimes in clusters of no more than five. Two really good flushes of flowers are produced in the season, each with plenty of blooms to make a memorable splash of color.

★★★

PLANT PROPERTIES

Shape and Size

The canes that are produced exude with strength and vitality. A free-growing plant that branches out, creating a substantial bush. Expect to see it grow to between 4 and 6 ft (1.2 and 1.8 m) tall, with a width of 2½ to 3½ ft (75 cm to 1.1 m).

Position

It will grow just about anywhere in the garden. Avoid areas of shade, which encourage it to grow taller in search of additional light.

Hardiness

Although it is very vigorous, it does not enjoy cold areas.

FOLIAGE PROPERTIES ★★★★★

Color

The dark green leaves are abundant, large and finished with a dazzling gloss. There is plenty of leaf to give good coverage, which makes it an imposing spectacle.

Health Check

Resistant to assault from most diseases most of the time. Blackspot may break down its defences in the second half of the season.

Garden Uses

Rose beds and gardens anywhere that height is required.

OVERALL ASSESSMENT ★★★★

✔ A fine color on a plant that is well behaved in most situations.

✖ The color that the flower fades to spoils the look. The plant can be excessively tall.

Savoy Hotel (Integrity)

Bush Rose (Hybrid Tea)

FLOWER PROPERTIES ★★★★★

Color

Light pink, a pure color unadulterated by any foreign pigments. The only exception is on the outer petals, which retain a green tone but are soon hidden as the flower opens. The flowers keep their true color, resisting any effort the sun makes to fade them and impervious to all but the heaviest rain.

Shape and Size

Round plump buds that are full of promise. Intricate and numerous rows of petals are arranged in wonderful symmetry, producing a flower with a perfectly formed center. There are so many petals that the flower keeps its shape for days on end, eventually opening to 3½ in (9 cm) across with 50 petals.

Scent

Not a strong perfume, but a light rose and spice aroma.

Production

Flowers are produced either as single blooms or in small clusters of no more than five, and the plant teems with blooms. It makes a great attempt to fully cover itself with bloom giving weeks of gardening pleasure. Provided the first flush is deadheaded and the plant is fed, there will be an equally fine second blooming.

PLANT PROPERTIES ★★★

Shape and Size

A variety that produces an agreeably shaped bush, well rounded and dense, with many branches. Growing to 3½ ft (1.1 m) tall and 2½ ft (75 cm) wide it is a useful garden plant.

Position

Good results in any position except heavy shade.

Hardiness

A tough and vigorous performer worth trying even in cold regions.

FOLIAGE PROPERTIES ★★★★★

Color

There is a lot of foliage on plants; the leaves are an average size. Starting out as a ruby red color, they grow to be mid green with a matte finish.

Health Check

High resistance to most ailments, but blackspot may gain a foothold under stress.

Garden Uses

Will add color to any rose bed or border.

OVERALL ASSESSMENT ★★★★

- ✔ The consistent size and quality of the flowers.
- ✖ The color is inoffensive but not inspiring; a good perfume would help.

Silver Anniversary (Karen Blixen)
Bush Rose (Hybrid Tea)

zone 7–8

FLOWER PROPERTIES ★★★★

Color

White. Uncomplicated simplicity with no subtle shades and variations.

Shape and Size

Large buds with flowers opening to high-centered elegant blooms. With 35 petals and at up to 3 in (8 cm) across the flowers look good for an extended period.

Scent

A light spice scent.

Production

For a hybrid tea this rose gives one of the most intense early displays. A large quantity of flowers cover the plant with abandon. A solid performance late in the season leaves little to complain about.

PLANT PROPERTIES

Shape and Size ★★★★

A robust plant that creates an imposing strong bush. With a tidy, rounded shape and plenty of stems, the plant looks substantial, growing to around 4 ft (1.2 m) tall and more than 2½ ft (75 cm) wide.

Position

It likes sunlight, so avoid shady positions.

Hardiness

Survives well in most regions but avoid the coldest.

FOLIAGE PROPERTIES ★★★★

Color

The plant is covered with big, dark green, glossy leaves. There are plenty of them, giving a lovely contrast to the white flowers.

Health Check

Overall a fine performer. Disease will not have any major or detrimental effect unless the plant is under stress.

Garden Uses

Formal rose gardens, beds and borders.

OVERALL ASSESSMENT ★★★★

✔ The total ease and reliability of the plant and flower.

✖ It lacks the "wow" factor that stops us in our tracks.

The McCartney Rose

Bush Rose (Hybrid Tea)

FLOWER PROPERTIES ★★★

Color

A mid to deep pink: not a complex color – one of its attractions is its purity. This is not the best flower to withstand rain damage.

Shape and Size

The flowers are strikingly large, with the classical high-pointed center of the hybrid tea. Their 40 petals are put to great effect as the flower opens to 4 in (10 cm) across.

Scent

The real reason to grow this variety – strong, sweet and beautiful.

Production

Enough flowers to give a lot of pleasure, but production is on the shy side compared to many other modern roses. Late season flowering is quite good.

PLANT PROPERTIES ★★★★

Shape and Size

Grows with enthusiasm to 4 ft (1.2 m) tall and 2½ ft (75 cm) wide, a bush that is full of promise. There is adequate growth to make a good foundation to display the flowers.

Position

Not one of the best in a shady site.

Hardiness

Survives well in most regions, but not very hardy in the coldest.

FOLIAGE PROPERTIES ★★★

Color

There is a lot of leaf, dark green with a slightly darker tint from the reddish spectrum.

Health Check

If conditions are against, it is likely to suffer an attack of powdery mildew. Prevention or cure will be needed.

Garden Uses

Best in rose beds or borders.

OVERALL ASSESSMENT ★★★

✔ The perfume will give unbridled pleasure.

✖ The health record gives cause for concern. It would be nice to have a few more flowers.

Warm Wishes

Bush Rose (Hybrid Tea)

FLOWER PROPERTIES ★★★★★

Color

A confection of sweet pinks, salmons and a dash of yellow. A delightful flower, resilient in sun and rain.

Shape and Size

Blessed with the most pure and uncomplicated flower shape. This is how a rose should be. The flower may have only 35 petals but they are used with devastating effect to create and keep that perfect rose shape. Up to 4 in (10 cm) across.

Scent

Combination of sweet rose and spice.

Production

The flowers come in small clusters that produce a sequence of well-sized perfect blooms. The repeat flowering is good, resulting in a plant that exceeds expectations by producing so many flowers.

PLANT PROPERTIES ★★★★

Shape and Size

There is a strength and dominance to the plant. It says "look at me, I'm wonderful." Bushy, dense and even in its growth, it may reach 4 ft (1.2 m) tall and 2½ ft (75 cm) wide.

Position

It will excel in all but the shadiest sites.

Hardiness

Slightly tender – advisable to protect it in cold climates.

FOLIAGE PROPERTIES ★★★★★

Color

The leaf is on the dark side, but no less attractive for that. There will be a good covering, even low down on the plant. A strong leaf in proportion and harmony with the showy plant.

Health Check

With a good health record there is little trouble if the plant is not under stress.

Garden Uses

Perfect for rose beds, borders and gardens.

OVERALL ASSESSMENT ★★★★

✔ A fine performer that will please the most demanding gardener.

✖ A little vulnerable in cold conditions.

shrub roses

Armada

Shrub Rose

FLOWER PROPERTIES ★★★★

Color

Very pink. Not a color to include in an area of restful pastel shades. This is a pure strong sugary pink that can be seen from a distance. The color is stable in all weather conditions. The petals are firm and robust, which helps them to resist wind and rain damage.

Shape and Size

The buds are rounded and small. One of the wonders of nature is how such large petals can come from such a small bud. There are only 10 petals, opening flat and showing the yellow of the stamens, contrasting brilliantly with the pink flowers.

Scent

Light with a hint of musk combined with the rose scent.

Production

This is where we get our enjoyment. Clusters of up to 35 buds will open over a period that extends into weeks, not days. Excellent at repeat bloom late in the season if you deadhead the early blooms. In full flower a canopy of bloom completely covers the top of the plant.

PLANT PROPERTIES ★★★★

Shape and Size

A really robust grower. The branches from the base will be thick and strong. It takes into the second or third season to become a dense bush and at this stage you will begin to see its true beauty. It will grow from 4 to 6 ft (1.2 to 1.8m) tall, and 3 or 4 ft (1 to1.2 m) wide.

Position

As with all roses, it will perform best in a good position but this is one to try in the more challenging sites. It is one of the toughest so expect good results in time.

Hardiness

Give winter protection in very cold areas.

FOLIAGE PROPERTIES ★★★★

Color

May be accused of having "plain" foliage: light emerald green, shiny and attractive.

Health Check

Renowned for good health, so ideal for beginners.

Garden Uses

Makes a great, colorful hedge; gives color in a mixed border.

OVERALL ASSESSMENT ★★★★

✔ The health and strength of the plant, quantity of flower.

✖ The color can be a bit harsh in some circumstances.

Ballerina

Bush Rose (Shrub)

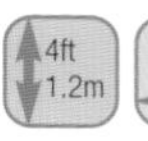

FLOWER PROPERTIES ★★★

Color

Soft, light pink around the outer petals, which pales to a white center – a combination reminiscent of apple blossoms. As the flowers age they will adopt a stronger pink shade. Flowers are unaffected by wind or rain but in very strong sunshine they lose some of their beauty towards the end of their lives.

Shape and Size

Individual flowers are tiny and struggle to reach 1 in (2.5 cm) across. Opening from tiny light green buds they will be fully open, fresh and delightfully pretty in no time at all. There are just five petals surrounding the yellow stamens in the center of the flower.

Scent

Not a variety that is selected for nasal appeal, as there is virtually no scent.

Production

Initial blooming commences a little late in the season, when many other roses are more than half way through their first flush. However, it is worth waiting for. The clusters of flower buds are massive, creating flower heads of well over 50 blooms, all opening in a sequence to produce a mass of delicate color for weeks and weeks. The effect is more like a hydrangea than a rose.

PLANT PROPERTIES ★★★★

Shape and Size

This is an easy plant to grow. It will naturally produce many basal shoots, giving a lovely bushy foundation to hold the striking flower heads. Expect a minimum height of 4 ft (1.2 m) and a width of 3 ft (1 m).

Position

This variety is strong, it will grow in any fertile soil, but select a light position with some direct sunlight. If it is too shady flowering will be too late. Avoid very windy positions.

Hardiness

There is very little that nature can provide to upset this one.

FOLIAGE PROPERTIES ★★★★

Color

Leaves are light green, appearing in groups of five, seven, nine and on odd occasions 11. They are relatively long and narrow, but in sufficient quantity to make the plant well furnished.

Health Check

Has no terrible vices. There may be attacks of powdery mildew in the second half of the season.

Garden Uses

Works well as an individual plant or wonderful in a mixed border.

OVERALL ASSESSMENT ★★★

✔ The gift to share so many flowers with us is awesome.

✖ A little late to begin flowering. In hot weather the old flowers are unattractive until deadheaded.

Bonica

Bush Rose (Shrub)

FLOWER PROPERTIES ★★★

Color

Bright and cheerful, a simple rose pink. The color is stable throughout the life of the flower. There are small variations of color within the petal: it has a slightly lighter reverse while the center of the flower is a little deeper.

Shape and Size

Round buds open quickly to reveal an uncomplicated bloom with 15 petals. Wide and flat, about 2½ in (6 cm) across, the flower is as simple in form as it is in color.

Scent

You will only appreciate any perfume if your nose is more sensitive than mine.

Production

The plant will be festooned with flowers. It has a long flowering period and the initial burst of flower will cover the plant and continue to do so for several weeks. Spectacular.

PLANT PROPERTIES ★★★★★

Shape and Size

This plant forms a dense dome, rounded and even, producing myriad thin stems that will hold flowers all over its domed shape, blooming from just above ground to the top of the plant. Ultimate size varies according to conditions and pruning; expect it to be in the range of 3 to 4½ ft (1 to 1.4 m) tall and 2½ to 3½ ft (75 cm to 1.1 m) wide.

Position

Grows in fairly shady spots as well as sunny positions.

Hardiness

As with many pink roses, it is very hardy. Worth trying in all locations.

FOLIAGE PROPERTIES ★★★

Color

Leaves are mid to light green, on the small side, but numerous. It is a pity that such a fine variety does not have more striking foliage.

Health Check

In most conditions health is good. Powdery mildew can be a problem in hot, dry periods. Plant in a position with good air circulation.

Garden Uses

In borders, beds or hedges where a splash of color is required.

OVERALL ASSESSMENT ★★★

✔ Easy to grow and ridiculously productive.

✖ The color is a bit boring, unless you want a plain pink.

Canary Bird

Bush Rose (Shrub)

FLOWER PROPERTIES ★★★

Color

Here we have another simple uncomplicated color. No combination of shades, just an intense bright yellow that remains the same throughout the life of the flower.

Shape and Size

With regard to flower size, the word small comes to mind. To continue the theme we get small buds, small flowers – only five petals – opening to no more than 1 in (2.5 cm) across.

Scent

Sorry, nothing to enjoy in this department.

Production

It may be the first rose to bloom in the season but it does not repeat later. The flowers are delicately held along the length of the branches and are produced on tiny stalks on the old wood. Where the plant makes new stems, these will flower in future seasons but not in their first season.

PLANT PROPERTIES ★★★★

Shape and Size

With regard to size we have a different theme – big. The canes from the base may shoot up to 8 to 10 ft (2.5 to 3 m). Mature dimensions can be up to 12 ft (3.7 m) tall and 10 ft (3 m) wide. The shape is divine: the long branches grow up and then arch gracefully downwards.

Position

With this amount of vigor any position is fine but do give it plenty of room.

Hardiness

Tough in nearly all regions. As it is tall it may suffer in windy sites.

FOLIAGE PROPERTIES ★★★★★

Color

The leaves are light green and have an unusual feathery appearance, closely spaced along the stem. The first impression is that they are fern-like. Good to use in flower arrangements – one of the few roses that has a pretty leaf.

Health Check

Here we have a variety of rose that is pretty indestructible. Good resistance to plant ailments makes it easy to care for.

Garden Uses

Plant it only if you have a big space, at the back of a mixed border or as a specimen plant.

OVERALL ASSESSMENT ★★★★

✔ Early flowering and pretty foliage.

✖ Short flowering period.

Constance Spry

Shrub Rose (Shrub)

FLOWER PROPERTIES ★★★★★

Color

Light pink in all its stages, be it a young bud or fading flower. The color is restful and tones down stronger colors in mixed plantings.

Shape and Size

Round buds open to supply blooms packed with petals. Curling and reflexing in orderly beauty, the 80 petals provide a wide flower of 3 in (8 cm) across. Good in all weather except heavy rain.

Scent

This is a flower that looks as if it should have perfume, and it does – a wonderful strong rose scent.

Production

The early flowering is a delight. Clusters of flowers adorn the bush, spaced at intervals that create a good cover. Enjoy the early flush, for there will be little later in the season.

PLANT PROPERTIES ★★★

Shape and Size

Grows to a bush of up to 8 ft (2.4 m) tall and 3 ft (1 m) wide. It is too tall and thin for many uses and is susceptible to wind damage. The canes are long and whippy and in some areas may need support.

Position

Plant only in areas with good levels of light.

Hardiness

Survives well in most regions.

FOLIAGE PROPERTIES ★★★★★

Color

The leaf is mid green without the polish we see on so many modern roses. There is a good quantity of leaf overall, apart from the lowest part of the plant.

Health Check

Usually holds its own against disease until late in the season.

Garden Uses

Mixed borders or shrub borders are best.

OVERALL ASSESSMENT ★★★★

✔ The flower is a delight of delicacy and form.

✖ The habit of getting too tall, and poor late season flowering.

Cornelia

Shrub Rose (Shrub)

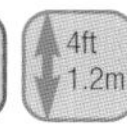

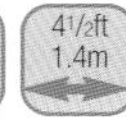

FLOWER PROPERTIES ★★★

Color

Pink with undertones of peach. This is one of the roses that always exceeds my expectations. It is a simple blend of pinks, yet every year when it blooms my reaction is the same – I'd forgotten how beautiful it is.

Shape and Size

Little plump, round buds open to neat flowers containing 30 petals. Around 2½ in (6 cm) across, the blooms combine a gentleness with elegant charm.

Scent

An enjoyable perfume; a sweet musk is the usual conclusion.

Production

The early flush of flower is the best, although in a good season late flowers can be prolific. The flowers are clustered, forming a pretty canopy of bloom over the plant.

PLANT PROPERTIES ★★★

Shape and Size

Grows into a rounded shrub, with a multitude of branches making a dense bush. It is good at producing an even and attractive plant. Mature dimensions vary according to conditions and pruning but expect a minimum height of 4 ft (1.2 m) and it can get to 6 ft (1.8 m) tall. The width will be between 3½ and 4½ ft (1.1 to 1.4 m).

Position

Best to plant in a favorable position; it certainly needs good light.

Hardiness

This rose will struggle in colder regions.

FOLIAGE PROPERTIES ★★★

Color

Light green color with a nice amount of gloss. The leaves are a good size but can be a little sparse on the plant.

Health Check

Powdery mildew is the main enemy. Grow in sites and conditions to limit the damage that can be caused by powdery mildew.

Garden Uses

Best in mixed borders or shrub rose gardens.

OVERALL ASSESSMENT ★★★★

✔ Combination of charm, scent and initial flowering.

✖ Foliage is not the best and repeat bloom can be poor in some seasons.

Flower Carpet (Floral Carpet)

Ground Cover Rose (Shrub)

FLOWER PROPERTIES ★★★

Color

This rose is unfortunate in having a color that I dislike, so I may not be very nice about it. It is a deep pink, which always looks as if it is fighting to stay pink, with bluish purple hues trying to distort the color. To be fair, other people like the color. For me it is too harsh.

Shape and Size

The flowers are small, which for this variety is fine. They open from rounded buds and have about 25 petals. The petals retain a pretty concave shape as the flower opens to about 1 1/2 in (4 cm) in diameter. It has good tolerance of wet weather.

Scent

No joy in this area as there is no appreciable aroma.

Production

One of the more prolific flower producers. Flowers are produced along the stems in clusters which are close to each other and become a sea of bloom. Capable of repeat blooming through the season; there are enough flowers to create a strong impact.

PLANT PROPERTIES ★★★★★

Shape and Size

The branches of this ground-cover rose will start by growing upwards and outwards from the crown of the plant. As they lengthen they begin to arch down, ending up as a mass of intermingled stems. Growing to a height of between 2 and 3 ft (60 cm to 1 m) and a width of 4 to 6 ft (1.2 to 1.8m) it will produce impenetrable ground cover.

Position

Good in any area, even heavily shaded.

Hardiness

It grows successfully in any area, so give it a go in cold tough locations.

FOLIAGE PROPERTIES ★★★★★

Color

The foliage is the best feature of this variety. The leaves look to be coated in wax, are fairly dark green and radiate good health. Leaves are produced at close intervals along the stem, which helps it to create good ground cover.

Health Check

One of the roses to receive top marks in this area. If growing conditions are good there should be no ailments.

Garden Uses

Great for banks and slopes that you don't want grass on. Good in tubs and planters.

OVERALL ASSESSMENT ★★★★

✔ Outstanding health and freedom of flower.
✖ The color leaves a little to be desired.

Gertrude Jekyll

Bush Rose (Shrub)

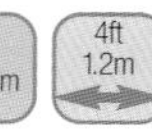

zone 6–7

FLOWER PROPERTIES ★★★★★

Color

A deep pink with intense depth. It is not a color that varies much during the life of the flower. Only in hotter conditions does the flower begin to fade.

Shape and Size

The buds grow to be fat and plump before they open. It takes a while for the flower to become fully open, as there are so many rows of petals, all arranged to perfection. The flowers are big; it is not unusual to see them 4 in (10 cm) across, and with more than 75 petals.

Scent

Don't get too close in case the scent overpowers you. Strong, sweet and intoxicatingly delightful.

Production

The flowers come in clusters, with the center bloom flowering first. This will be the largest of the flowers, the remainder of the cluster being smaller. There are plenty of flowers but never a mass to cover the whole plant at once. Repeat blooming is reasonable late in the season.

PLANT PROPERTIES ★★★

Shape and Size

Established plants tend to be a bit leggy – there is a penchant for the lower half of the plant to be short of leaves, just a display of thorny old stems. According to the climate and pruning regime the expected height is from 4 1/2 to 7 ft (1.4 to 2.2 m) and a width of 3 to 4 ft (1 to 1.2 m). The plant will be more upright than bushy.

Position

Give it a site with plenty of sun and good ventilation.

Hardiness

Suitable in all but the coldest regions.

FOLIAGE PROPERTIES ★★★★

Color

The color is mid green with a faint purple hue and matte finish. Leaves are plentiful on the upper half of the plant, sparse at lower levels. Although the leaves are large they never look very robust, which may be because of the color.

Health Check

Powdery mildew is the main concern. Unless preventative action is taken the plant will suffer.

Garden Uses

An asset wherever perfume is required and the height can be accommodated.

OVERALL ASSESSMENT ★★★★

✔ The perfume and shape of the flower.

✖ Health and foliage could be better.

Graham Thomas (English Yellow)

Shrub Rose (Shrub)

zone 6–7

FLOWER PROPERTIES ★★★★★

Color

Primrose yellow with a hint of gold – a rare color in a shrub of this type. It is a yellow with a lot of good qualities: it remains constant in all conditions, the petals are strong, resisting any damage that the weather may try to inflict.

Shape and Size

Another rose that will produce big, round buds, full of promise. Buds opens slowly, providing a flower of ever more beauty as it progresses. The petals retain a concave shape, as if protecting the center of the flower, and there are too many rows to count. With up to 75 petals crowded into a flower measuring up to 4 in (10 cm) across, we can gaze into this bloom with appreciative wonder.

Scent

A distinct and pleasing perfume but not overpowering.

Production

Coming in clusters of up to seven blooms, which open over an extended period, there is good continuity of flower. An able provider of bloom in the late season.

PLANT PROPERTIES ★★★

Shape and Size

While the rose will grow well, it is likely to become overly tall, making stems vulnerable to wind damage. Producing a good number of stems in a large plant gives it a dominant physical presence. Reaching between 5 and 9 ft (1.5 and 2.7 m) tall, but only 3 and 4 ft (1 and1.2 m) wide, the size of this plant will vary according to local growing conditions.

Position

This rose must have an area with good light and some direct sunlight. Shade will make it too tall and weak.

Hardiness

While the plant grows with vigor, it is not so well suited to the coldest sites.

FOLIAGE PROPERTIES ★★★

Color

Rich dark green, large and well polished. Plenty of leaves gives the plant a good appearance, although they are less dense lower down where stems may become a bit bare and woody.

Health Check

This will not be one of the first to suffer from ill health. If there is an infestation around it will fall victim to either blackspot or downy mildew, but it has good overall resistance.

Garden Uses

Ideal at the back of beds and borders where height is required.

OVERALL ASSESSMENT ★★★★

✓ The best of the taller yellows, a strikingly beautiful flower.

✖ The growing habit can make it too tall, subject to wind damage, with too many flowers at the top and too few lower down.

Jacqueline du Pré

Bush Rose (Shrub)

FLOWER PROPERTIES

Color

Almost white, sometimes with a pink flush. One of the flowers' unusual features is the red stamens in the center. A resilient flower that maintains its good looks in adverse conditions.

Shape and Size

Outstandingly pretty yet very simple. There are only 10 petals in the flower. It starts as a long conical bud, quickly opening to a flat flower where all the petals reflex and curve. Flowers average 3 in (8 cm) across.

Scent

For such a delicate flower, the power of the perfume is a wonder. A combination of musk and lemon.

Production

Few roses are capable of producing more blooms per year. They are borne in clusters, opening in a controlled sequence to maximize the life of every cluster. Flowering starts early, sometimes four weeks before other bush roses. The repeat is rapid. Three flushes per season are to be expected.

PLANT PROPERTIES ★★★★

Shape and Size

A wide and bushy specimen. Average dimensions will be 4½ ft (1.4 m) tall by 3½ ft (1.1 m) wide. It produces an impenetrable matted mass of stems that work hard to support the mass of flowers.

Position

A hardy plant that will accept any position, even places where there is shade.

Hardiness

Possesses a strong constitution; it is worth trying in either hospitable or hostile positions.

FOLIAGE PROPERTIES

Color ★★★

The leaf has a matte finish and a mid to dark green shade. It is not one of the attractive leaves – more of a functional item than a beauty accessory.

Health Check

There is little disease where growing conditions are managed well. If there is a problem, it will be blackspot in the second half of the season.

Garden Uses

It is so amenable and versatile that it will enhance any garden.

OVERALL ASSESSMENT

✔ Extremely long flowering; scent and flower beauty. ★★★★

✖ Let down by the quality of the leaf and susceptibility to blackspot.

Marjorie Fair (Red Ballerina, Red Yesterday)
Bush Rose (Shrub)

  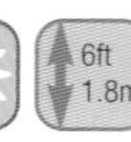 

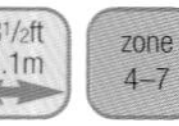

zone 4–7

FLOWER PROPERTIES ★★★

Color
The two distinct colors are cerise and white, divided into concentric circles. The central inner section of the flower is white, and the outer ring cerise, making a bold effect. Flowers endure any amount of wet weather, but in high intensity sunlight they fade badly as they age. Deadheading keeps the appearance attractive.

Shape and Size
There will be hundreds of tiny, light green buds on this plant. Each will open into a bloom of no more than 1 in (2.5 cm) wide. They have only five petals arranged wide open in a circle.

Scent
In spite of the quantity of flowers produced, the scent is negligible.

Production
Produced in vast clusters, tightly packed together, there is the potential to have a complete sea of blooms covering the plant. Repeat blooms well in the late season.

PLANT PROPERTIES ★★★★

Shape and Size
A thicket of stems are produced from the base of the plant. It will be dense and impenetrable, growing 4 to 6 ft (1.2 to 1.8 m) tall and 2 1/2 to 3 1/2 ft (75 cm to 1.1 m) wide.

Position
Anywhere in the garden – in hot areas avoid full sun.

Hardiness
Renowned for its hardiness and worth trying in any region.

FOLIAGE PROPERTIES ★★★★★

Color
The leaves are small and numerous. With a mid to light green shade and matte appearance they are not the most attractive. Best considered as being functional rather than beautiful. They fulfill the functional role with aplomb, clothing the plant in a dense and even green coat.

Health Check
As healthy as it is hardy. Impervious to most attacks, with the exception of powdery mildew late in the season.

Garden Uses
Hedges and mixed borders will exploit its strengths.

OVERALL ASSESSMENT ★★★★

✔ Ease of culture and productivity.

✖ The color of the old flowers can deteriorate if you don't deadhead.

Mme Isaac Pereire
Shrub Rose (Shrub)

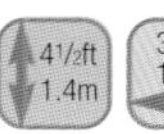

FLOWER PROPERTIES ★★★★

Color

There is richness in the deep crimson to purple color. It is one of those roses that are tactile – you have to feel the petals as well as look at them. They feel soft, which is lovely, except it means that they are subject to rain damage, which may spoil the flower by making brown spots on the petals. Petals discolor as they age, taking on a bluish hue.

Shape and Size

Large cupped flowers up to 4 in (10 cm) across with around 50 petals arranged in a neat symmetrical intricate pattern. Each is a work of art to be savoured and enjoyed.

Scent

Heady and intoxicating on a balmy day. Another variety that should be in the top ten.

Production

There are just enough flowers, but more would be nice. They are borne in small clusters spread around the plant, without covering it densely. A pleasing first flush is followed by an even more sparse second flush.

PLANT PROPERTIES ★★★

Shape and size

A plant of significant stature, bold and tall, growing to at least 6 ft (1.8 m) and 4 ft (1.2 m) wide. The plant produces plenty of stems, making a dense shrub.

Position

Requires reasonable light, so avoid medium to heavily shaded areas.

Hardiness

It is worth trying everywhere for the scent alone. Protection required in colder regions.

FOLIAGE PROPERTIES ★★★

Color

Mid green foliage can have a slight grey undertone. The leaves are not the strongest aspect, less attractive than many other varieties.

Health Check

An acceptable level of health, but it needs watching. Both powdery mildew and blackspot can pay visits and remedial action will be required to prevent heavy infestations.

Garden Uses

At the back of borders – as it flowers mostly at the top, shorter plants in front will not hide many blooms.

OVERALL ASSESSMENT ★★★

✔ The flower will satisfy three senses: sight, touch and smell.

✖ Not healthy enough to survive without attention and work.

Nevada

Nevada (Shrub)

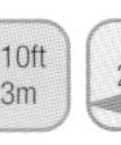

FLOWER PROPERTIES ★★

Color

Fluctuating between cream and white, with the occasional flush of pink. The pink appears as the flowers are finishing. They begin cream and fade to a near white before petal fall.

Shape and Size

Measuring around 2 in (5 cm) across when fully open, they are pretty little flowers with five petals. A fine example of how something simple can combine both beauty and elegance.

Scent

A light but a perceptible offering that has hints of citrus.

Production

Only one decent flush of flower – one spectacular display, with nothing in the fall. Buds are produced all over the plant, from almost ground level to the top – a sight to relish.

PLANT PROPERTIES ★★★★

Shape and Size

Imagine a plant that is up to 10 ft (3 m) tall and 8 ft (2.5 m) wide. It is large, the branches arch, tier after tier of them making a neat rounded gigantic bush. The lowest branches just brush the ground, the highest grow straight up the middle of the plant.

Position

If you have a big space, even in shade, it will fill it for you.

Hardiness

Worth trying in exposed or cold sites and excellent in favourable positions.

FOLIAGE PROPERTIES ★★★

Color

Small leaves abound. They could be at closer intervals on the plant, which could look better furnished with leaf, but there are enough to cover most of the stems. Light in color, matte in appearance, they do a workmanlike job without venturing into the realms of beauty.

Health Check

This is a strong rose. Few ailments attack this monster of a plant.

Garden Uses

Ideal as a specimen plant or for the back of borders. It must have space to thrive.

OVERALL ASSESSMENT ★★★

✔ That one flush of flower is enough to earn it a place in any large garden.

✖ The size is a drawback, as is the inability to produce a second flush of flower.

Rubrifolia (Rosa glauca)

Shrub Rose (Shrub)

FLOWER PROPERTIES ★★★★★

Color

The most insignificant flower in this book. It is a variety that earns its inclusion by a multitude of attributes other than its flower. The flower is light pink, graduating to white. This rose also produces a veritable cascade of bright red hips in fall.

Shape and Size

The flowers are small; less than 1 in (2.5 cm) across, with five petals. They are pretty in their own way, but not really significant. The hips are rounded but not quite a perfect sphere. They will be about 1/2 in (1 cm) across.

Scent

The flowers are gone before you have chance to check it out and, if you do, there is very little there.

Production

The plant is festooned with flowers early in the season. It will not repeat and the flowers last only a few days. The hips turn red in very late summer or early fall. Like the flowers they will also cover the plant, but unlike the flowers, they remain visible and enjoyable for a long time. It is not unusual for hips to still be present at Christmas.

PLANT PROPERTIES ★★★

Shape and Size

Big in all dimensions. It will produce a woody thicket all on its own. With arching branches up to 9 ft (2.7 m) tall, and a width of up to 6 ft (1.8 m), this is a specimen that requires space. It will not respond happily to attempts to confine it.

Position

Provides satisfaction wherever it is planted.

Hardiness

Worth trying in all regions.

FOLIAGE PROPERTIES ★★★★★

Color

Here we find another reason for growing this variety. The leaf is small for such a large plant, and the color unusual. It retains a purple tint throughout the season. During the first half in particular the foliage is very pretty – it is an asset in flower arrangements.

Health Check

Few health problems here. If the plant is afflicted with any ailment it has enough vigour to survive the attack.

Garden Uses

The foliage and hips can be enjoyed as a specimen or at the back of a mixed border.

OVERALL ASSESSMENT ★★★★

✔ The leaf and hip give this interest when other roses may not be at their best.

✖ It needs a lot of space. The flower is only fleeting.

Sally Holmes

Shrub Rose (Shrub)

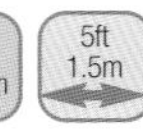

FLOWER PROPERTIES ★★★★★

Color

Cream and honey are the dominant colors. They blend together with a tendency to fade to white as the flower ages. It is a pretty fade, not one that disfigures or detracts from the color of the younger flowers.

Shape and Size

Big, wide, open flat flowers with just five petals, up to 4 in (10 cm) across.

Scent

Light, fresh and enjoyable perfume – not a lot from individual flowers, but adequate collectively.

Production

Big clusters of blooms with more than 40 buds to a cluster. The plant will be covered in clusters and in full flower there is nothing but flower on show. Flowers open sequentially in the cluster giving an extended flowering period. Repeat flowers in the late season.

PLANT PROPERTIES ★★★

Shape and Size

A substantial bush in all dimensions. The growth is sturdy, holding the heavy flower heads proudly. It reaches between 4 1/2 and 8 ft (1.4 and 2.5 m) tall, with a width of between 3 and 5 ft (1 and 1 1/2 m).

Position

It will grow in sunny or shady sites.

Hardiness

There is a strength and resilience to the plant, but it requires protection in the coldest regions.

FOLIAGE PROPERTIES ★★★★★

Color

The plant would look better if it was clothed with more leaves, which can become sparse on the lower branches of the plant. The leaves are attractive, although they would be a better foil for the flower if they were a darker shade of green.

Health Check

Strong resistance to disease, but powdery mildew can put in an appearance late in the season.

Garden Uses

Mixed borders, hedges and as a specimen plant.

OVERALL ASSESSMENT ★★★★

- ✔ The outstandingly beautiful flower, which is also good as a cut flower.
- ✖ The foliage is mediocre, and the color insipid to some people.

Scabrosa

Shrub Rose (Shrub)

FLOWER PROPERTIES ★★★★★

Color

Rich magenta with hints of purple. A color that will make you stop and look, to fully appreciate its beauty. Yellow stamens in the center of the flower create a bold contrast. In the late season there will be tomato-red hips for added color.

Shape and Size

The flowers open into large flat blooms, the five petals opening wide to make the flower over 3 in (8 cm) across. The hips are of equal stature, fleshy, plump and rotund. They will be at least 1 in ($2^1/2$ cm) in diameter.

Scent

The flower may not have many petals, but it has abundant perfume. Strong, sweet, a real rose fragrance.

Production

Flowers in clusters strategically placed over the bush make a prolific early flowering. Unusually for a variety with a showy display of hips, these will be followed by a reasonable late season flush. Hips will mature to tomato red in very late summer, and will be there to enjoy until well into winter.

PLANT PROPERTIES ★★★

Shape and Size

A mature bush will be big and wide. A matted confusion of branches make the bush rounded in shape, and up to 8 ft (2.5 m) tall by 5 ft (1.5 m) wide. Each branch is covered in very fine sharp thorns, more like prickly hair than normal thorns.

Position

A plant that is able to contend with any position you give it.

Hardiness

Try in cold zones as well as more temperate areas.

FOLIAGE PROPERTIES ★★★★★

Color

The foliage is distinctive, a light green with a wrinkled appearance. It looks hard wearing and covers the plant with an impenetrable mass of leaf. As the leaves fall they turn yellow.

Health Check

Full marks for its ability to resist any attack.

Garden Uses

At the back of borders, hedges or as a specimen plant.

OVERALL ASSESSMENT ★★★★

✔ Bullet-proof health and hardiness; great hips.

✖ A few more flowers that lasted longer would be a big improvement.

The Fairy
Bush Rose (Shrub)

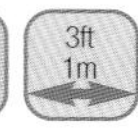

FLOWER PROPERTIES ★★★★

Color
A soft, warm rose pink, steadfast regardless of the weather – sun and rain make little impression.

Shape and Size
Small flowers are 1 1/2 in (4 cm) across with 35 petals. Flowers are rounded with petals that crinkle and curl prettily into the center.

Scent
Best described as absent.

Production
This rose is completely awesome in its ability to flower. It becomes a mound of pink with flowers everywhere. A little late to start flowering, but worth every minute of the wait.

PLANT PROPERTIES ★★★★

Shape and Size
An individual rose that will grow to about 3 ft (1 m) tall. It forms a rounded mound, as wide as it is tall. The branches grow up and then arch gracefully down, allowing it to flower from the ground upwards.

Position
A versatile plant, happy in either sun or partial shade.

Hardiness
Give protection in the coldest areas for a good display.

★★★★

FOLIAGE PROPERTIES

Color
Another charming feature of this variety. The leaves are a fresh, light green with a deep polish. They are small and produced in a density that covers the plant completely.

Health Check
Nothing to worry about. An occasional attack of powdery mildew is about all you will see withthis hardy rose.

Garden Uses
Borders, patio tubs and mixed plantings. ★★★★

✔

OVERALL ASSESSMENT

✖ It is unusual, very colorful and grows easily. It likes to grow wide and will get shabby if it isn't pruned.

climbing roses

Albéric Barbier

Climbing Rose (Rambler)

FLOWER PROPERTIES ★★★

Color

The effect is overwhelmingly cream. Combinations of off whites and light yellows produce a bright, light effect. There is very little color fade, as the original flower is a combination of light shades. The only adverse quality is that it suffers from bruising and marking in wet conditions.

Shape and Size

The flowers open from rounded buds to flat blooms. They are pretty as individual flowers, as the petals are crammed into dense circles of unfurling beauty. The fully open flower will be up to 3 in (8 cm) in diameter, containing around 70 petals.

Scent

Not renowned for its perfume but possessing a light, musky scent.

Production

Produces flowers in abundant clusters early in the season. If most of the old flower heads are removed there will be a few blooms later on.

PLANT PROPERTIES ★★★

Shape and Size

A vigorous climbing plant, it can grow up to 25 ft (7.5 m) tall, covering a width of 15 ft (4.5 m). It produces long climbing canes that are easy to train against a structure. The canes are long and flexible, making it suitable to train in a position that requires a long, low plant (like a 4 ft/1.2 m wall) as well as in traditional tall spaces. Not a variety to grow in a small space: unless you have an area in excess of 120 sq ft (11 sq m), it's best to skip this one.

Position

Requires a light position, with partial sunlight. Good soil needed to get the best results.

Hardiness

Will grow in most areas. In cold climates, position where it is protected from strong winter and spring winds.

FOLIAGE PROPERTIES ★★★★

Color

The leaves are dark in color with a sheen that makes them an attractive feature. They are medium in size and will often be produced in groups of seven, nine or even 11 leaves.

Health Check

A variety that will shake off most attacks, as long as it is fit and strong with good growing conditions.

Garden Uses

Grow up or along any structure that is big enough to accommodate its vigorous nature. It may be grown into old trees.

OVERALL ASSESSMENT ★★★

- ✔ Good health and ease of care. The flowers are beautiful individually and effective en masse on the plant.
- ✖ Not a good second flowering season and the blooms may be damaged by wet weather.

Bridge of Sighs
Climbing Rose

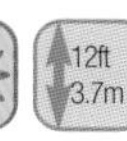
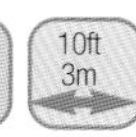

zone 6–7

FLOWER PROPERTIES ★★★★

Color

Gold infused with peach tones is a rare color in a climber. The color remains stable as the petals age; a little more of the peach tones comes through in hot conditions.

Shape and Size

Small buds open quickly into simple flowers with 10 petals. One of the unusual features of the flower is the way the petals are frequently pointed, giving a charming shape to the wide open flower. The blooms average 2 1/2 in (6 cm) in diameter.

Scent

Surprisingly strong for a small flower; sweet, with hints of honey and lemon.

Production

Flower production can be summed up in one word – prodigious. Clusters of flowers start early in the season and repeat with astonishing rapidity.

PLANT PROPERTIES ★★★★★

Shape and Size

A climber with long canes that are easy to train if you allow them to ripen before you bend them too much. It produces plenty of basal shoots to use to create a good framework. The lateral shoots that bear the flowers are not too long and quick to grow. You will be able to train the canes to anything from 6 to 12 ft (1.8 to 3.7 m) tall and 6 to 10 ft (1.8 to 3 m) wide.

Position

It will be happy in an open position. Partial sunlight is also acceptable.

Hardiness

Not suited to colder regions where it will be susceptible to winter frost damage.

FOLIAGE PROPERTIES ★★★★

Color

Initially leaves are deep red, which is an attractive stage. They turn dark green with a non-gloss shine.

Health Check

When the plant is in full flower it requires copious amounts of water to maintain health. If allowed to become stressed it is vulnerable to blackspot.

Garden Uses

Wherever a climber is required, except in heavy shade or a north-facing site.

OVERALL ASSESSMENT ★★★★★

✔ A great color for a climber, with good scent.

✖ It requires plenty of food and water to get the best results.

Compassion
Climbing Rose

FLOWER PROPERTIES ★★★★★

Color

A combination of shades, including pink, salmon and peach tones, which all combine to produce a pretty confection of color. Color varies with daylight length and sunlight intensity, becoming more salmon-colored with long, warm days.

Shape and Size

Large plump and rounded buds open into young blooms with a pointed center. As they progress to large cupped flowers, the full array of colors blends together. Large flowers up to 4 in (10 cm) across, with around 45 petals.

Scent

Exquisite perfume, really strong from each individual flower. With blooms massed on a plant, the scent is almost overpowering.

Production

A repeat-flowering climber having two highly rewarding flushes of flower. Spectacular in full bloom, managing to flower from low down to the top of the plant.

PLANT PROPERTIES ★★★★

Shape and Size

A climber with reasonable vigor. It will not go wild and can be trained easily. The stems are slightly stiff, meaning it is important to train them in the period after they begin to ripen, but before they become too stiff.

Position

Happy growing up any structure, but do not plant it facing north.

Hardiness

Thrives in all conditions.

FOLIAGE PROPERTIES ★★★

Color

The leaves are large and dark green. There are plenty of them to create a good background to complement the flowers.

Health Check

In the late season it may suffer from a light dose of powdery mildew or blackspot. It is not overly susceptible to these ailments but maintaining good growing conditions reduces the chance of disease.

Garden Uses

Up any structure that requires a climbing plant.

OVERALL ASSESSMENT ★★★★

- ✔ Has a better perfume than almost any other repeat-flowering climber.
- ✖ Needs to be cosseted and given good conditions to prevent foliage troubles.

Della Balfour (Royal Pageant, Desert Glo)

Climbing Rose

FLOWER PROPERTIES ★★★★

Color

A color of interest and beauty. A gentle meeting of oranges and yellows, the colors of fire, which combine in a restful, complementary way. As the flower ages it becomes infused with pink.

Shape and Size

Large buds open to reveal long petals and initially blooms use this length of petal to form elegant young flowers. These become round cupped blooms of 30 petals. Each flower can be up to 4 in (10 cm) across when fully open.

Scent

Endowed with a subtle spicy musk perfume.

Production

Flowers in groups of three or five. Smaller clusters than many climbers but the extra size of the blooms helps to give good coverage. It repeats well late in the season.

PLANT PROPERTIES ★★★

Shape and Size

A climber with moderate vigor, making it an option for confined spaces. The canes are sturdy and less pliable than average for a climber. It is ideal to train as a traditional fan shape. The mature height will be between 7 and 11 feet (2.2 and 3.3 m), spreading 6 to 9 ft (1.8 to 2.7 m) wide.

Position

Requires some direct sunlight. Avoid heavy shade, and sites facing northwest, north or northeast.

Hardiness

Will be happy in all but the coldest regions.

FOLIAGE PROPERTIES ★★★

Color

Starting off a rich red, the leaves progress to mid green hue at maturity. They are large robust leaves that offer a good foil to the flower color.

Health Check

Subject to suffering from blackspot when under stress, so keep well fed. Good culture will reduce the severity of any attack of blackspot.

Garden Uses

On walls, fences or up trellises.

OVERALL ASSESSMENT ★★★★

✔ The colors are wonderful in a climber

✖ Not the hardiest or the easiest to train.

Dublin Bay
Climbing Rose

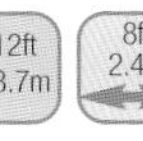

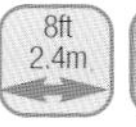

FLOWER PROPERTIES ★★★

Color

Deep red, deepest at the outer edge of the petals. Unlike many reds, the color is stable as the flower ages, even in bright sunlight. It may suffer from some spotting in wet weather.

Shape and Size

The buds are conical, opening to reveal a flower that develops quickly into a large open bloom of 4 in (10 cm) across. There are only 20 petals, but they last well and provide pleasure for days on end.

Scent

A disappointment as this red has virtually no perfume.

Production

In clusters of five or seven, blooms open in sequence to provide a good duration of flower. Repeating well, there will be plenty of flowers throughout the season.

PLANT PROPERTIES ★★★★

Shape and Size

Restrained and controllable growth by the standards of the average climbing rose. It generates a plethora of stems that provide good cover for the structure it is grown against. An anticipated height of 8 to 12 ft (2.4 to 3.7 m) and 5 to 8 ft (1.5 to 2.4 m) wide.

Position

A tough plant, although not highly vigorous. It will grow in most positions, even shady sites.

Hardiness

No special treatment required. Worth trying in all regions.

FOLIAGE PROPERTIES ★★★★

Color

The leaves are on the dark side, which is a pity, since a dark green leaf is not the best color to show off a deep red flower. The leaves are large and plentiful giving good coverage.

Health Check

Acceptable resistance to the ailments that nature throws into the garden, but not perfect. The main concern is blackspot and, in some seasons, a little powdery mildew. Best to avoid planting in areas that will exacerbates these problems.

Garden Uses

Over walls, fences and low structures, including pergolas and arches.

OVERALL ASSESSMENT ★★★

✔ That wonderful color, which is repeated throughout the season.

✖ Weak on the health front.

Françoise Juranville

Climbing Rose (Rambler)

FLOWER PROPERTIES ★★★★

Color

There is an enduring warmth to the color, a simple rose pink that pleases the eye and sparks a feeling of well-being. Unfortunately the color is not perfect: it will fade in intense sunlight. Even worse, heavy rain turns some petals to a soft brown decaying pulp.

Shape and Size

Bursting from plump round buds flowers are full of charm and promise. As the bud opens it keeps on delighting us with more and more petals, which curl and reflex prettily, with the smallest ones crowded into the center of the bloom. The wide-open flower measures up to 4 in (10cm) across.

Scent

The welcome sweetness of a traditional rose perfume wafts from the flowers.

Production

Flowers appear on short lateral stems along the main branches. They are plentiful, giving a good cover of bloom. The only downside is that there is not a strong showing after the first flush, just sporadically flower.

PLANT PROPERTIES ★★★★★

Shape and Size

A plant that always exhibits plenty of vigor. The climbing shoots can grow up to 10 ft (3 m) and have good flexibility, making them a pleasure to train against a structure. Once the initial framework of the plant is established, it will fill in with strong lateral growths. Growing up to 15 ft (4.5 m) tall by 12 ft (3.7 m) wide, it is able to create a stunning impact.

Position

While it will be happy in most positions, reasonable light levels are needed for it to excel.

Hardiness

A hardy specimen, but does not enjoy the coldest regions without protection from winter winds.

FOLIAGE PROPERTIES ★★★

Color

Mid green in color with a well-polished surface. The color of the leaf works very well and there are plenty of leaves to provide a backdrop to the flowers.

Health Check

Considering the age of the variety it is remarkably good at repelling the ailments that can attack roses. Depending on conditions there may be some powdery mildew or blackspot, but not heavy infestations.

Garden Uses

Grow as a climber on any structure in a light position. If you can find it as a weeping standard (Tree Rose), it makes a beautiful plant.

OVERALL ASSESSMENT ★★★

- ✔ The combination of old-world charm and robust nature. Stunning when grown as a weeping standard.
- ✖ Failure to have a decent second flush of flowers.

High Hopes
Bush Rose (Climber)

FLOWER PROPERTIES ★★★★

Color
The result is a pink flower but the ingredients that make the color are complex. A range of colors from a creamy pink to a light salmon pink blend together to make a pretty bloom. The petals are firm and resist damage from wind, sun or rain.

Shape and Size
Long petals provide a classical high-centered bloom as the bud begins to open. Opening into a bloom of 2½ in (6 cm) across, 25 petals form a long-lasting circular flower.

Scent
An enjoyable and reasonably powerful perfume.

Production
Produces clusters of up to five blooms that all last well, resulting in a long flowering period. A good second flush of flowers late in the season, makes this a rewarding climber.

PLANT PROPERTIES ★★★★

Shape and Size
Producing vigorous, long climbing stems, it grows into a large climbing plant between 10 and 18 ft (3 and 5.5 m) tall and 6 to 12 feet (1.8 to 3.7 m) wide, depending on conditions and pruning. The stems are not too thick, making them pliable and easy to train.

Position
A robust performer that will grow anywhere.

Hardiness
Worth trying in all areas, although some protection may be required in cold regions.

FOLIAGE PROPERTIES ★★★★

Color
Starting red and turning to mid green, the leaves are close together and large. Plants are well furnished with foliage, making a good green background for the flowers.

Health Check
A variety with very good disease resistance. If it is growing without any stress it will remain healthy.

Garden Uses
Great on walls, fences and large arches or pergolas.

OVERALL ASSESSMENT ★★★★

✔ There are no obvious faults, it is competent in all respects.

✖ Competent in all respects, it excels in no respects.

Kiftsgate (Filipes Kiftsgate)
Climbing Rose (Rambler)

FLOWER PROPERTIES ★★★★★

Color
White, with prominent yellow stamens in the center of the flower.

Shape and Size
Tiny buds open to tiny flowers. They have five petals and measure no more than 1 in (2.5 cm) across. Flowers remain clean and bright until the petals fall off, resisting rain damage with ease.

Scent
Individual flowers have a tiny amount of scent. A plant covered in them fills an area of the garden with a sweet combination of vanilla and banana.

Production
Flower clusters are large and impressive. There may be over 100 buds in a big cluster. This rose starts to flower later than most varieties, providing bloom when others are finishing their first flush of flower. The flowers open over a period of a few weeks. Unfotunately, there is no worthwhile late flowering.

PLANT PROPERTIES ★★★

Shape and Size
This is about the most vigorous climbing rose there is. It will grow up to 35 ft (10.5 m) tall and 25 ft (7.5 m) wide. It can be kept a bit smaller, but do not try to restrict it to a small area – it likes to fill in big spaces. The long stems are very pliable and easy to train.

Position
Try covering a shed or fence. This rose can be grown into trees and conifers, adding flowers where they are not expected.

Hardiness
If it won't grow, your conditions are very testing.

FOLIAGE PROPERTIES ★★★★

Color
Light in color, the leaves are in groups of five to 13 leaves. The plant produces them at remarkably close intervals, making a dense blanket of foliage.

Health Check
The constitution is tough. Nothing appears to stop its advance; if disease attacks the plant it will continue to grow regardless.

Garden Uses
Only suitable where there is adequate space. Grow into trees and hedges for additional interest.

OVERALL ASSESSMENT ★★★★

✓ Easy to grow, will cover awkward and difficult areas with verve.

✖ Shorter flowering period than we would like. Needs a lot of space.

Little Rambler
Climbing Rose (Climber)

FLOWER PROPERTIES ★★★

Color

The buds are light pink when they are young and begin to open. As the flower develops it will pale to a soft pearl shade, and in the final stage the bloom will be white before petal fall.

Shape and Size

Rounded buds are small, but plump. They open to semi double flowers, no more than 2 in across. The petals are tightly packed as they unfurl from the tight bud, and then the yellow center of the flower smiles out from a flat open flower.

Scent

Only a light perfume, a waft of rose scent can be found on a warm summers evening.

Production

Unlike the ramblers of old, this is a repeat flowering variety. It will provide two good main flushes of flower. The flowers come in clusters, so although the individual flowers are small the dense clusters will ensure that there is a big splash of color for a long time.

PLANT PROPERTIES ★★★★★

Shape and size

As the name suggests, it is little for a rambler. The height will be between 6 and 8 ft tall, growing up to 7 ft wide. It has all the attributes of a rambler, long slender stems that are easy to train, plenty of vigor and a robust constitution, but all this is within a small and manageable framework.

Position

Grow in any location except heavy and dense shade.

Hardiness

A variety that is tough, much tougher than the slender stems would have you imagine.

FOLIAGE PROPERTIES ★★★

Color

The leaves are small, in perfect proportion with the plant. Light to mid green with a well polished attractive appearance. There are just enough of them to make a good background to the flowers.

Health Check

As with many vigorous plants the overall health of this variety is good when growing well. With a plant in less than ideal conditions and some stress, then you will have to protect it from both powdery and downy mildew.

Garden Uses

A rewarding rose to grow on fences, walls or small pergolas.

OVERALL ASSESSMENT ★★★★

✔ All the charm and beauty of an old rambler in a compact and manageable plant.

✖ While there are lots of flowers the color is a little weak with some further fade.

Mermaid

Climbing Rose (Climber)

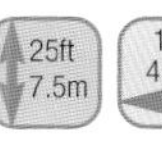

zone 7–8

FLOWER PROPERTIES ★★★★

Color

Light primrose yellow. There are occasions when it seems a little pale, but it is always pretty. In most conditions there is a perceptible, detrimental change to the color as the flower ages.

Shape and Size

With just five petals and a flower frequently more than 3 in (8 cm) in diameter, it is easy to imagine that the individual petals are large. When fully open the flower is a real beauty, exhibiting deep yellow stamens.

Scent

While there is not a lot of perfume, there is a musky aroma from a plant covered in bloom.

Production

With clusters spread evenly all over the plant there is no shortage of bloom, and it flowers for a long period. As individual blooms are so large it is still striking even when there are not many flowers on the plant.

PLANT PROPERTIES ★★★★

Shape and Size

A climber with plenty of vigor. The stems that it produces are long and flexible. However, care is needed, as the wood is more brittle than many other roses and if you try to bend it too much it will snap. Growing to between 15 and 25 ft (4.5 and 7.5 m) tall and 8 to 15 ft (2.5 to 4.5 m) wide this is a substantial climber.

Position

Somewhere with good light and some direct sunlight.

Hardiness

With protection it will be safe to try in cold areas.

FOLIAGE PROPERTIES ★★★

Color

Leaves are dark green and lustrous. It produces a good quantity of leaves low down, so there should be no problem with legginess.

Health Check

Look forward to a trouble-free experience. Any problems will be late in the season.

Garden Uses

In beds and borders, or as an individual accents to make a splash.

OVERALL ASSESSMENT ★★★★

✔ Simplicity and beauty of the flowers.

✖ Questionably hardy in cold positions; predilection towards downy mildew.

Morning Jewel
Climbing Rose (Climber)

FLOWER PROPERTIES ★★★

Color

A very bright and almost shocking sugary pink, with a tiny white eye. It stands out from a distance and polarizes opinion – you either love it or hate it. It is impervious to the ravages of rain or excess sun, retaining almost all its color until the petals fall.

Shape and Size

Plump buds open to produce flowers with about 20 petals. Blooms are wide, 3 in (8 cm) across, with the petals retaining a concave shape for most of the flower's life.

Scent

Best described as absent. This rose is for visual enjoyment.

Production

The first flush of flower in the summer is wonderful. Clustered in sets of five buds, the flowers open to cover the entire plant. All you see is a wall of color, no leaf, and no gaps. The repeat bloom is not so dense and can be improved by deadheading after the first flush.

PLANT PROPERTIES ★★★★

Shape and Size

A climber that is restrained in its growth. It may be kept from 6 to 10 ft (1.8 to 3 m) tall and 5 to 9 ft (1.5 to 2.7 m) wide. The plant generates enough canes to train into a good fan shape. The wood is stiff, so do not try to bend it too much when training it.

Position

Happy in either sun or shade, so any position is suitable.

Hardiness

This rose is a tough cookie. Worth trying in all areas.

FOLIAGE PROPERTIES ★★★★★

Color

Light to mid green and very shiny. There is plenty of foliage and it looks great behind the flowers in early summer.

Health Check

This rose has always had a good reputation for health. In adverse conditions it can be afflicted by downy mildew.

Garden Uses

On walls, garden structures or fences. It will even perform well on north-facing sites with poor light.

OVERALL ASSESSMENT ★★★★

- ✔ Hardiness and ability to perform in difficult positions.
- ✖ Requires deadheading for a good second flush.

New Dawn

Climbing Rose (Climber)

FLOWER PROPERTIES ★★★★★

Color

Very gentle and restful, the most tender mother-of-pearl pink. In the bud the color may be a little deeper, lightening as the bloom opens. There is a risk of damage from heavy rain.

Shape and Size

Flower structure is somewhat informal. The petals may be concave or convex – they are a mixture, a success of random organization over structured symmetry. There are only 25 petals in each flower, which rarely exceeds 2 1/2 in (6 cm) in diameter.

Scent

Traditional rose scent – a wonderful wafting perfume from a plant in full flower on a warm summer evening.

Production

Clusters of five flowers produced evenly over the plant means there is no shortage of bloom. The early flowering is better than late in the season.

PLANT PROPERTIES

Shape and Size ★★★

This is an enjoyable climber to grow. The canes are long, easy to train to the horizontal or vertical. Growing to a size that is controllable, between 9 and 15 ft (2.7 and 4.5 m) tall by 6 to 10 ft (1.8 to 3 m) wide, with plenty of growth to make a substantial framework to support the bloom, it has all the essential features of a climbing rose.

Position

Tolerant of aspects facing any four points of the compass, even in fairly shaded locations.

Hardiness

Although the flower may look delicate, the plant is robust and happy to tackle all but the most severely challenging environments.

FOLIAGE PROPERTIES

Color ★★★

There is an abundance of leaf, in a mid green that works well with the flower color.

Health Check

Generally a trouble-free rose. In adverse conditions either blackspot or downy mildew may attack.

Garden Uses

On any structure in the garden, especially good for arches and pergolas.

OVERALL ASSESSMENT ★★★★

✔ Unrivaled ability on arches and similar structures. Very pretty in bloom.

✖ It would be better with more foliage and an increased capacity to repel disease.

Penny Lane
Climbing Rose (Climber)

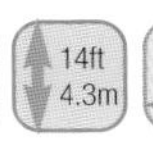

FLOWER PROPERTIES ★★★★★

Color

A delicate shade often described as honey champagne. There is a little splash of pink in the early stages of the flower, which later fades towards white.

Shape and Size

Round buds open to become large flowers well endowed with petals, maybe as many as 70. The flowers can reach 3 1/2 in (9 cm) in diameter, with large petals around the outside, smaller shorter petals crammed into the center. With all these petals it is a long-lasting flower, able to withstand all but the heaviest rainstorms.

Scent

Individual blooms have a moderate scent with a musk base. En masse the plant covered with bloom perfumes the evening air.

Production

This has to be among the most productive climbers. It creates clusters of flower, often exceeding 11 buds each. The clusters open over a long period, and it produces a succession of clusters late into the season. There will be flowers for many weeks every season.

PLANT PROPERTIES ★★★★★

Shape and Size

A very well-behaved climber. Growth is adequately strong for most uses, but not too vigorous, reaching between 9 and 14 ft (2.7 and 4.3 m) tall and 6 to 10 ft (1.8 to 3 m) wide. The canes are supple which makes them easy to train on most structures.

Position

Tolerant of a wide range of conditions and worth trying in all sites, even those with shade.

Hardiness

Hardiness is one of the virtues – with protection it will thrive in the coldest areas.

FOLIAGE PROPERTIES ★★★★

Color

Producing a veritable blanket of leaf along the stems, the plant offers a contrasting background to the lightly colored flowers. The leaves have a reassuring dark green color and deep sheen.

Health Check

Able to withstand most ailments without too much problem. In some conditions powdery mildew may make an appearance late in the season.

Garden Uses

On any structure or vertical surface that requires covering.

OVERALL ASSESSMENT ★★★★★

✔ The pleasure of a rose that will always perform well.

✖ The color is too pale for some people.

List of Suppliers

There are many excellent suppliers for rose plants, some serving just a local community, and others that ship nationwide or internationally. Here are some that are worth trying, but you should always be willing to try others, as new rose nurseries are regularly starting up.

Don't forget to search on the internet for more information on growers and suppliers. In addition to the suppliers listed here there are Garden Centers to visit. Good garden centers will provide strong and successful plants.

USA AND CANADA

Edmunds Roses
6235 SW Kahle Road
Wilsonville, Oregon
USA 97070-9727
Tel: 888-481-7673
www.edmundsroses.com

Heirloom Old Garden Roses
24062 NE Riverside Drive
St. Paul, Oregon
USA 97137-9715
Tel: 503-538-1576 Fax:
www.heirloomroses.com

Jackson & Perkins
1 Rose Lane
Medford, Oregon
USA 97501
Tel: 1-877-322-2300
Fax: 1-800-242-0329
www.jackson-perkins.com

Pickering Nurseries, Inc.
670 Kingston Rd.
Pickering, Ontario
Canada L1V 1A6
Tel: 905-839-2111
Fax: 905-839-4807
www.pickeringnurseries.com

UK

R. Harkness & Co. Ltd
Hitchin,
Herts. SG4 OJT
Tel: 01462 420402
E-mail: harkness@roses.co.uk
Web: www.roses.co.uk

James Cocker & Sons
Rose Specialists
Whitemyres,
Lang Stracht,
Aberdeen, Scotland
AB15 6XH
Tel: No. 01224 313261
Fax: No. 01224 312531
www.roses.uk.com

C&K Jones
Golden Fields Nursery,
Barrow Lane,
Tarvin, Cheshire
CH3

Fryer's Roses
Manchester Rd.
Knutsford, Cheshire
WA16 0SX
Tel: 44 01 565 755 455

GERMANY

Rosen Union
61231 Bad Neuheim-Steinfurth
Steinfurther Hauptstrasse 25
Germany

W. Kordes Sohne
Rosenstrasse 54
Klein Offenseth
Sparrieshoop 25365
Germany

DENMARK

Martin Jensens Planteskole
Stavelsager 9
Skovby
5400 Bogense
Denmark

HOLLAND

Jan Timmermans VOF
Rijksweg 42
6049 GW Herten
Holland

Roparu Rosen VOF
Ien de Nej Erf 32
5861 CG Wanssum
Holland
Tel: 31 478 532 841
Fax: 31 478 531 771

Fa. Jac Verschuren - Pechtold
Kalkhofseweg 6a
5443 NA Haps
Holland
www.verschuren-pechtold.nl

BELGIUM

Fa. Willem van Herreweghe
Nieuwstraat 50
B-9260 Serskamp
Belgium
Tel: 32 093 690 176
Fax: 32 (0)93 661 957
www.willemvanherreweghe.be

FRANCE

Edirose
RN6/Chesnes
38070 St Quentin Fallavier
France
Tel: 04 74 94 04 36
Fax: 04 74 95 54 16

NEW ZEALAND

Matthews Nurseries Ltd
Wanganui
www.rosesnz.co.nz

Index

Page numbers in italics indicate an illustration in the Choosing and Growing section, but note that all roses (listed under *Rosa*) have an illustration also.

Acknowledgments

All photographs supplied by Steve Wooster except on the following pages.

29, 31 and 33 Holt Studios/Nigel Cattlin

21, 30, 44, 49, 63, 71, 79, 101, 102, 103, 108, 111, 115, 116, 119, 123, 124, 131, 138 Philip Harkness

Zone Map of U.S. and Canada

A plant's winter hardiness is critical in deciding whether it is suitable for your garden. The map below divides the United States and Canada into 11 climactic zones based on average minimum temperatures, as compiled by the U.S. Department of Agriculture. Find your zone and check the zone information in the plant directory to help you choose the plants most likely to flourish in your climate.

Zone 1	Below -50°F (Below -45°C)
Zone 2	-50° to -40°F (-45° to -40°C)
Zone 3	-40° to -30°F (-40° to -34°C)
Zone 4	-30° to -20°F (-34° to -29°C)
Zone 5	-20° to -10°F (-29° to -23°C)
Zone 6	-10° to 0°F (-23° to -18°C)
Zone 7	0° to 10°F (-18° to -12°C)
Zone 8	10° to 20°F (-12° to -6°C)
Zone 9	20° to 30°F (-6° to -1°C)
Zone 10	30° to 40°F (1° to 5°C)
Zone 11	above 40°F (above 5°C)